D1485416

2000-11-65

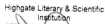

A FOOL IN THE FOREST

LEONARD CLARK

A FOOL IN
THE FOREST

Illustrated by RICHARD SHIRLEY SMITH

LONDON : DENNIS DOBSON

Printed in Great Britain by
East Midland Printing Co. Ltd.
Bury St. Edmunds, Suffolk.

CONTENTS

I was born in the Channel Islands but brought up in the Forest of Dean, that ancient land of woodlands and coalmines between the rivers Severn and Wye which, by some continuing miracle, has escaped the worst effects of the Industrial Revolution.

I lived in the Forest for a quarter of a century, for all my childhood and adolescent years in fact, within sight of the Cotswolds and the Black Mountains of Wales. It still has my allegiance.

At a later stage of my life I worked in London, in Devon, and in Wharfedale in the West Riding of Yorkshire, and now again in London. The collection of essays which follow, several of which have been broadcast, are the record of my experiences in those places, and of some of the people I have met. They are, in some part, fragmentary chapters of autobiography, though I recognize that a collection of essays is not a single complete work.

I have most to say about the Forest of Dean, that place of my happy, if uncertain, youth—those far off, shining years of forty years ago, when I thought with Traherne that ". . . all things abided eternally as they were in their proper places".

"A fool, a fool! I met a fool i' the forest,
A motley fool."

As You Like It. vii.12.

I THE RUINED FOREST

I WAS brought up in a forest, which means, if you like forests, that trees become part of you, your brothers and sisters, as it were. The trees of my forest became a part of me, so that even now I must live where trees are; I pale when I hear that one is to be cut down. I become a different creature when I move among trees; their woody spirit seems to enter into me. I inherit their silence; I breathe more freely in a forest than on any windy moor or exposed sea shore.

There was one wood, a small part of the larger Forest of Dean, called the Chestnuts Wood, which first took its place in my childhood geography when my uncertain baby steps brought me to the top of the hill near my home to look out over the spreading West Gloucestershire countryside. There was the Severn, a quick, star-caught eel in the near distance, and, far away on the skyline, the Cotswolds, like strange embattlements blotting out the rest of the world from my young eyes. And there, to the left, only a few fields away it seemed, lay the Chestnuts Wood, at peace on a noble hill. I thought it looked like a giant's umbrella. Certainly it invited me to explore it and this I was to do many times before it was lost to me for ever.

There had always been trees on that enchanted hill. The earliest maps of the district showed a thick wood. As a boy, I imagined Silures crouching low in their war paint waiting for the Roman legions to cross over Severn. My ready imagination planted Robin Hood and his secret company there, William of Normandy hunting the red deer and, at another stage of my childhood, peopled it with English gnomes and fairies. When I grew up, and came to the understanding and appreciation of these things, the Chestnuts Wood had become a lovely and enduring stretch of forestland beneath broad skies.

In time, I learned that the Chestnuts Wood had been re-planted in 1812 after a fall of timber during the Napoleonic wars. They planted seventy-four acres of it, avenues of oak and chestnut, spreading round the hill from the south, to Popes Hill in the north, and along the Greenbottom road between Tibbs Cross Farm and Greenway Farm. Trees from this wood had been rolled to the dockyards for the building of ships which had borne the brunt of cannonades at the Nile and Trafalgar. Their ancestors had fought the Spaniards; in 1812, oaks were being planted to replenish the stocks of timber for the king's navy. Forty years later they would be meeting the Russians in the Crimea. But the fury of the old wars died away, the wooden walls rotted into decay, and the Chestnuts Wood went on growing until, by the time I knew it, the hill had become a solid phalanx of tall trees, standing trunk to trunk, branches interwoven, a thick, impenetrable net, almost blotting out the sight of sun and stars.

I got to know every inch of the Chestnuts enclosure—the springs, farms, cottages, and boundary stones, as well as the trees. My mother used to take me to see a cousin of hers who lived on the far side of the wood from us. We used to visit him in the time of plums and cider, walking leisurely and happily through the wood to his squat cottage hidden among bird-loud orchards. I could plot every ride and track, I was on familiar terms with the ruddled sheep which grazed at the edge of the wood; it did not take me long to discover the loneliest places. There were days in those boyhood summers when I lay, in idleness, on my back in bracken, listening to soft pigeons moaning overhead, and to the clicking sounds from hidden insects, warming their stiffened wings in the sunshine. When the dew began to fall, I watched for badgers and early foxes on the prowl. In those enraptured days, the light filtered through the tops of the trees, falling on me, and on my young hopes. And there, ringed by regiments of foxgloves or battalions of bluebells, I watched summer pass, and autumn come with browning fern, cold, talking streams, and ripe chestnuts falling soundlessly from prickly husks. There was no more solitary spot in the wood than the highest point of it. And there I would sit, my back against a tree, surrounded by silence, the earth still warm, the woodpeckers interrupting sleep. So I dreamed my boyhood away. In autumn, too, I used to meet the long timber wagons rattling through the wood, scoring deep squelchy ruts in the tracks, with the carters singing and the patient horses striding along, harness jingling. I used to pass the time of the day with some of the woodmen I knew, Frank Edwards, Sam Cowmeadow, Jack Fisher and Willy Hayward who, no doubt, wondered what I was doing there.

And, in winter, I again made my way to the frosted woods. Then, apart from the occasional scuffling bird, there would be no life there. Squirrels were sleeping somewhere, foxes had gone to earth, spiders were locked up in winter quarters. But the Chestnuts Wood meant as much to me then as at its upspringing and fullness. Its emptiness, its strict economy, the sudden suspension of its life, matched my adolescent moods. How often have I shattered December quietness by plunging a vulgar foot into the freckled ice that covered the wagon ruts.

I left home in my early twenties. But the map of the Chestnuts Wood, with Greenway Farm, Tibbs Cross, Badcocks Bailey and Morpeth Point, was indelibly written on my heart's memory. Two hundred miles away from the wood I used to lie awake at nights and imagine it at each season of the year. How many times have I dropped off to sleep to the sound of its fragile streams in my ears, and had a memory of sheep staring over the tops of the foggy ferns, and cock pheasants rasping overhead.

Whenever I went back home, the Chestnuts Wood was still there. I used to wave a greeting to it from the heights of my hill country. I walked into the valley, down over the fields, to pay my respects to the trees.

Then, in 1939, the war came. I heard rumours that many of the older oak trees were suffering from heart rot which was rapidly degrading them. I heard terrible whispers that the Chestnuts Wood might have to be felled.

And then, in the autumn of the first year of the war, I heard the news. It was contained in a letter from my mother. She had added an ominous postscript. "You'll be sorry to hear that they are cutting down the Chestnuts Wood." For the next few weeks I wrote to her daily asking to be told how the murder was proceeding. For murder it was to me. I thought of the woodmen's axes at their deadly work. I saw the great, grand trees toppling to ruin. I heard their dying screams. I had panting nightmares when the trees turned on me and accused me of treachery. The axes cut deep into my heart.

Not all the acres of oak and chestnut were cut down at once. Felling went on steadily, as timber was needed, throughout the years of the war. Mother died in 1940 and I went home to her funeral. When it was all over, I left the place at once; I could not bear to look at the nakedness of the Chestnuts hill and especially now she was gone who had loved the wood so well.

I knew, though, that many of my childhood friends were

grieving with me. Years after, Eric Johnson told me he used to turn his eyes away whenever he looked out over the valley so that he might not see how much farther the felling had gone. George Evans, who was a Crown woodman, shook his head sadly and said, "A terrible thing it is. But it had to be. Them old trees was rotted at their hearts." And Emmie Williams whispered through thin, tight lips, "I never go down there now, nor take the children. There's nothing to go for."

By 1944 the trees had all gone, except for one solitary strip of oak on the very top of the hill, on the Popes Hill side. In the summer of 1945 I went home again. I was determined to find out the worst for myself. And so I stood once again on my childhood heights and looked around me. There stood the jagged Cotswolds, the meadows of corn waving below, Severn glinting, the needle-points of the scattered churches, and, most comforting of all, the calm, white glory of Gloucester Cathedral tower. Yes, it was all there as it had always been. And then I turned my eyes to the left of the familiar landscape. There, to my horror, I saw a bald hill with just a thin ring of trees right on the top. My eyes flooded with tears. So this was all that remained of my Chestnuts Wood. Fate had tonsured the hill as if compelling it to do a penance. Seventy acres of forest had gone and, with it, I felt that my roots had been pulled up. I cannot begin to calculate how much of my life went with the destruction of those trees.

The hill was replanted in 1949 with oaks and conifers but, for me, it would never be the same again. Whatever bluebells might rise to fire its glades, whatever owls might come to hoot in its dark corridors, whatever new tracks might run from one end of it to the other, none of these would be mine.

It was the old people who grieved most of all. For them, the Chestnuts Wood had been mysterious, half-explored territory. "I always used to 'urry through the wood," said Granny Cresswell, "O, it was too ghostie for me. But now them trees is gone, I do miss 'em." And Frank Coneybeare, who used to walk the whole length of the wood twice a day to, and from, the colliery, confided in me, "When I was going home at night I saw the wood getting less. The trunks was piling up all round me like headless corpses. They was at it for a whole month. And then I went home another way." And Phil Nelson who lived in a cottage near the wood said, "Nelsons have lived in this cottage for over a 'undred years. Some of 'em helped to plant them trees to stop Boney. It was lovely getting up in the morning and seeing 'em there. Now there is only their stumps."

The last time I went home I saw the new wood. The baby trees had grown quite a bit. The hill did not look so cropped, so barren, so deserted. Everything looked tidier and much more ordered—like a plantation. So I took comfort in the thought that a wood, like the Chestnuts Wood, does not come to maturity in one man's lifetime, the trees do not shoot up overnight like dragons' teeth. Perhaps, I mused, my children's children would, one day, lose themselves in the undergrowth of this new wood, listen to summer birds, wander there in autumn and dream their dreams, as my forefathers and I had done before them. Yet, they would not know the wood I had known, nor catch any hint of my old melancholy, nor my desperation when the wood of my day had been conquered by those plundering axes. So do forests rise and fall from generation to generation. They have their magnificence and their ruin.

2 THE RIVER BANK

THE river was the Severn, four miles from my home. I had
known it for as long as I could remember, for mother often
used to take me to see it when I was quite a baby. As we lived
on the edge of a forest, water was a new and strange element
to me. I must have seen the river many times after that, and
played on its bank and dabbled in its summer waters. But it
was not until I was nearly 10, and about to go off to the
grammar school, that I really became aware of the river, and of
what it meant to me. Then I became one of its most ardent
worshippers (little knowing that it had, as a matter of fact, its
own Roman river god, by name, Nodens).

The walk to the river was nearly all downhill, and through
some of the loveliest countryside in the neighbourhood. We
passed fields of white, grazing sheep, a village of sleeping
Georgian houses, quiet copses, an old British camp, with far-off

13

peeps of the river through gaps in the hedges. In spring, the banks between the cuttings were thick with violets and wind-flowers. Later those hedges had their trailing briars and old man's beard. But it seems to me now, so far away from it all, that the fields always had lambs and daisies, that every farm smelt of new-mown hay.

Suddenly the lane stopped where it joined the main road. This was the village of Newnham's High Street, and on the other side of it was the steep descent to the river. Its waters appeared round the bend with the same shock of surprise to me as the Israelites must have felt when they saw the Red Sea for the first time. So exciting was the prospect that I used to break into a jog-trot as soon as I knew I was getting near to the water.

I see myself again, on a day in late summer, a stocky little boy, legs and feet bare, face freckled, shirt open at the neck, morning-white tennis shoes dangling round my neck. There I am on the river bank, feeling very happy and cool, and look-ing out gladly over Severn. I am in love with the world. At my back rises a great red cliff, broken here and there by layers of grey shells, seeming to join the sky. On the top of this cliff stands the village church. I can just see a few of the grave-stones, and the tops of crosses and the eyeless heads of stone angels. There used to be a story that once in a while you could see coffins and a few bones sticking out of the cliff but it was never my good fortune to enjoy such a thrilling sight. The bank dips gently to the river. I lift up my eyes and see the further bank, across the mile or so of water, where cows are up to their knees and birds dive low to the mud. And beyond them, there is a church spire, a thin black wedge shooting out of the orchards. And to my left, there is the river still stretch-ing out of sight, a long reach of enchanted water, with trees and fields meeting the water's edge, old slipways, a pub, a cottage or two, and rotting boats. I feel the full happiness of it all still, a great sense of freedom, too, and the knowledge that I had inherited all the waters of the earth.

Yes, I remember the sun shining on Severn, on the bank, and on me. I wanted to race along that little stretch of warm sand and shingle, splash into the water, jump into the air, and shout. I used to wade into the water as far as I dared down the sloping shelf. The sun, the river, the air, the sand, possessed me. I thought nothing could ever spoil my delight. I was ten and everything was fine.

Nothing could keep me from the bank at the time of the Severn Bore. Then I would cycle on my old boneshaker, like a lunatic, down the hills to the river and stand, awed and tongue-tied, with other lunatics, as the great, high wall of water tore upstream, roaring at the sky. It was a sight which must have struck the ancient men who fished here with terror and fear.

And this same tide would bring the elvers, a glittering miracle every spring, the river swimming and cloudy with them, with everyone on the bank ladling them in, in their wriggling thousands, into every kind of receptacle from pint pot to tin bath. What an Easter harvest. The tiny, magical, black-eyed fish would soon be sizzling in every frying pan for miles around. I was wild with excitement when the milky mass floated my way and I could plunge my eager hands into the heart of the slimy tangle.

Once, after a high tide, as I was roving upstream, dreaming of Romans and Britons whose blood had mingled in Severn waters, I almost stepped on a dead sheep, a soggy bloated bag of flesh and wool that had been cast upon the bank and lodged in the hairy roots of a tree. I was so stricken I could not move. I had not seen death before in such hideous form. This, I thought, had been a lamb. It had once grazed peacefully on the tender grass of the Welsh mountains. Perhaps it had strayed from its fold and been swept away by night. I could imagine it struggling against the strength of the flood water. Already the flies were at work on it, already the face was losing its shape. It was horrible. I turned in my tracks, shaken to the

B

heart, and went back to the security of the cliff. I hated the
place.

But joy soon returned with the salmon fishers and their
seines, and the little skiffs that used to go bobbing gaily round
the cliff, and the apple blossom from the orchards farther upstream which rode the waves, floating coverlets of pink light
and shadow. And the church bells would no doubt be ringing
above, bob majors and triples, loud and clear across the water.
The boys would be courting the girls. The young corn would
be springing.

But that autumn came the incident of the ferry.

There was a man, a retired boat-builder, who used to ferry
people over, that is, whenever he felt like it, in his small tub
from the Newnham bank to the mud flats on the other side.
Everybody knew how treacherous and strong were the
currents in that spot, and how necessary it was for the right
time of the day to be chosen for the crossing. One afternoon I
was sitting, cross-legged, shoulders humped, with a friend on
the river bank. We were thinking our long thoughts and passing away the time by playing ducks and drakes. There was
nothing else to do. Then we decided to go over to the other
side, to Arlingham, where Tom Sayers, the boxer, was born.
It was low tide, so we had to wait a bit. But eventually the
short journey was over, and we were carried in turn in the
ferryman's arms, over the mud flats to the green bank above.
He stank of cider. On returning from the village in the evening, we had to wait the best part of an hour for the fellow to
turn up. We called and called and waved our arms. But in
vain. He did not come, and our spirits sank. The sun began to
set as we sat miserably on the bank watching the lights go
up, one by one, in the houses on the distant hills. Sometimes
we laughed and cracked jokes but it was all rather false. We
wondered what was being said about us in our homes, and
thought bitterly of the long four-mile pull up home in the
dark. Then an old woman joined us, gliding, as it were, out of

the dark. She was carrying two huge straw chips and wearing a man's trilby hat. She gave one look at us. "You look like the lost sheep of Israel," she chuckled. "And hasn't *he* turned up yet?" she barked. "I know where he'll be. In *The Sailor* I expect, guzzling cider as usual. You wait till I see him." Almost before she had finished speaking, we heard the sound of drunken singing coming over the dimming waters. The ferryman had turned up at last, but so full of liquor that he could barely stand up in his boat. And it had not made him very merry, either. He ordered us into the boat with cursings and mutterings. He said something about boys who ought to be in bed at that time of night. We sat in silence in the prow, cowed and frightened. The man and the woman then began to quarrel as she gave him the rough edge of her country tongue. A wind began to rise. The boat began to rock from side to side. Apprehensively we peered through the darkness at the home shore. Soon it was clear that he had missed the proper channel, and was incapable of rowing against the tide. We moved all too slowly downstream. Then it began to thunder and lightning and soon to rain. We thought every moment would be our last, that the boat would sink with the lot of us. And all the while, as we got more and more soaked, the man and the woman quarrelled. He lurched when once she got up to threaten him. After what seemed an age, we ran ashore in the mud on the other side, the best part of a mile from the village. Then we had to trudge along the bank and over some fields to get to the road. It was only when we had left the lights behind us and were well on our way, that we realised we had not paid for our ride. I still don't know why we were not all drowned.

But I did see a drowning once, and the river and its bank never felt the same after that. Mother and I were picnicking there one August bank holiday. We had strolled down over the fields and along the shady lanes in the early afternoon. The bank was crowded. Nearly all our friends were there. The small children were paddling and the babies were being dandled in the tiny, lapping waves. It was all innocent and peaceful. Severn was dazzling. I was talking to mother about what clothes I should have to wear at the grammar school. I think she was a bit disappointed that the outfit didn't include a mortar board. Suddenly there were shouts and frantic screams. Everybody on the bank jumped up, and many rushed down madly to the river. I stood where I was. Then I saw some men lift something out of the river and lay it on the sand. But I could not see what it was. Then somebody bawled out, "She's drowned. She's drowned." A small procession formed and the men trudged up the sand with the body of a dead girl. As they carried her up the sloping, cobbled patch into the village I caught a quick sight of her face. She was a girl I knew, a little older than me. I often used to see her about the town. She had a sad face, I used to think, and now I was looking at her face again, pale and bruised, and her hair soaking and tangled. It was awful. I was fascinated but repelled. This was far worse than the drowned sheep. With hot face and wild, beating heart I caught hold of mother's arm. We made for home, silently leaving the treacherous river behind us.

I learned much on that river bank. It had poetry and atmosphere. I like to think now that it had everything that was shining, glorious and happy. I try to forget the drowned sheep and the memory of that poor girl, but I cannot. I know now that my innocence had been assailed. I was ten and growing up.

3 THE BOXING MATCH

I WAS about twelve when I saw my first boxing match. It was a lightweight contest between Harvey Blanch of Ruardean and Stan Phillips of Drybrook; Ruardean and Drybrook are villages in the Forest of Dean.

Harvey Blanch was about the best boxer my part of the world ever produced. And he was my boyhood hero, the whole nine stone nine pounds of him. I was once out for a walk with my friend, Edgar, when I caught sight of Harvey on the other side of the road. "That's Harvey Blanch, the boxer," I said in an awed whisper, proud that it was I who had pointed him out to Edgar who had never seen him before.

"What, do you know him?" said Edgar. "My dad says he's a champion."

And on one Saturday afternoon I actually spoke to Harvey just outside Herbert Barter's fried fish shop. "Hello, Harvey," I said, and then bolted off.

The boxing match took place on the stage of the old Empire

cinema in my home town of Cinderford. It was a very special occasion, for as a rule, they only had films and turns on the stage—like men getting out of straitjackets and Red Indians lifting pianos with their teeth, and things like that. But on that autumn Saturday night the management put on a boxing match; and I made up my mind that I was going to see it. Of course, it was useless discussing the matter with my mother. And even if by some miracle she had agreed to my attendance, I had not got the money (front seats 5s., back seats 2s., standing room only, 1s.), and even if I had the money, they would not have let me in. When I told Edgar what was in my mind he laughed out loud and said, "You always was a bit potty. And what are you going to tell your mother when you get home at ten o'clock?" I had not thought that one out.

For about three weeks before the boxing match took place our town was plastered with bills. They were on all the hoardings and in every shop window. They announced in big black letters that Harvey Blanch, of Ruardean, late champion of the Herefordshire Regiment and holder of a belt, one of the most promising lightweights in Great Britain, had been matched to meet Stan Phillips, of Drybrook, who had never lost a contest and who had been itching for the past four years to get at Harvey. There was to be a silver cup for the winner, the gift of our local jeweller, and a purse of £20. The fight was to last for fifteen rounds.

At breakfast the following Saturday I politely informed my mother that I was going to chop a lot of wood for her that day, lift half a dozen rows of potatoes, and do any other jobs she had for me. She gave me a very odd look. The faintest of smiles spread over her face when I went on to tell her that a special meeting had been called, for that very evening, of our scout troop, which was likely to go on for three or four hours.

"And what would you lot be talking about for three or four hours?" countered my mother.

"Plenty," I nodded gravely.

As soon as I had finished all the jobs—to the great surprise of my mother—I went round to see Harry Knight. He was the "chucker out" at the Empire cinema, and a good friend of mine. Luckily Harry was in. I offered to sell programmes at the boxing match and, I went on, it might be a good idea if I wore my scout uniform. Harry did not think this was necessary and, in any case, informed me that there were not going to be any programmes. I made a number of other helpful suggestions but Harry had no use for my services.

I was about to leave his house in black despair when he suddenly called me back with the words, "Now you sit down there and listen to me. I got to be on duty all the time in case there's trouble, see. But if you'd care to nip out when the fight's nearly over and fetch me a pint of bitter from *The Lamb* I think I might squeeze you in at the back. So you bloody well come round to the side door not later than half-past six!"

I was out of the house in plenty of time that evening, in fact before mother could ask any more embarrassing questions. I had to wear my scout uniform, of course, and I prayed that I should not run into Willie Thomas, our scoutmaster. But, unluckily, on the way to the Empire I ran into Edgar.

"Here," he said, "where are you going in your scout clobber?"

"Special meeting of my patrol," I lied.

Edgar scowled, "Strange I never heard nothing about it."

I left him standing in the road. "And keep your silly mouth shut," I shouted as I pelted on down the hill.

I knocked on the side door of the cinema several times before old Harry came and let me in. He was in his shirtsleeves, sweating and swearing. They had already got the ring up on the stage and the gas lights were turned down.

"Now, you nip up into the gallery and hide yourself somewhere in the back," said Harry in a vague sort of way. "And

if any nosey parker asks you what you are doing here, you tell
him you are Harvey Blanch's nephew."

From a small window at the back of the gallery I could see
the crowds queuing outside. It looked as if the whole of the
Forest of Dean had turned up. There was a long line, stretching
from the road to the front doors of the Empire, of men in caps
and bowler hats, wearing silver watch chains and navy blue
suits, and of soldiers in khaki, home on leave from the war. It
was a warm evening and the sun, already setting behind the
distant blue Welsh hills, cast its shadows over the town. I
recognised some of the faces. There were lots of our local
tradesmen, chaps from the Gloucester regiment I had grown
up with, the manager of the bank carrying an umbrella, and,
most surprising of all, John Emery, our headmaster, and both
the churchwardens.

They began to let them in at half-past seven. They stormed
the entrances as if heaven itself were on the other side. The
crowd was thicker than ever. Both our policemen had turned
up now, with the sergeant. Parties were coming from all over
the place, by rail and horse brake, with a strong and noisy
contingent from Stan Phillips's village of Drybrook.

By eight o'clock the Empire was packed, and I was one of a
solid wedge of excited boxing fans all voicing opinions as to
how the fight would go, and all, apparently, with inside
knowledge. Harvey was clear favourite: most people seemed to
think that Stan Phillips, for all his reputed hefty right-hand
punch, would not go the distance. By now I was pressed tightly
up against the handrail of the gallery, and rather wishing I
had not come at all. The ring seemed an awful long way off.
I could not see Harry and felt a bit lost without him. I was
almost stifled by the clouds of tobacco smoke. The man on the
right of me smelled of meat and beer; he was one of the town's
butchers. He was smoking a short black cigar and every so
often he would clear his throat and spit. The man on the other
side was a complete stranger but of frightful appearance. He

had a boss eye which seemed to be permanently fixed on me and an iron hook for his left hand, with which, from time to time, he scratched his balding scurfy head.

Then Stan Phillips appeared, wearing an old mackintosh. There was a roar which echoed round the cinema, and a great wave of clapping. The men from Drybrook rose to their feet in a body and greeted their man. But this was nothing to the tumult which followed when Harvey Blanch stepped proudly into the ring already stripped for the contest. He looked wonderful. So tumultuous was his welcome that it seemed as if the roof would give way. From all over the house I heard shouts of "Good old Harvey", "Knock his block off, Harvey".

I have few memories of the boxing match itself. I remember both men slogging away, Harvey twice knocking Stan down, Stan making Harvey's nose bleed, the tobacco smoke getting thicker and thicker, the noise more deafening. The referee, a little man in white flannels, with black pomaded hair parted in the middle, found no favour at all from the Drybrook contingent. They shouted the most awful things at him and threatened to deal with him afterwards.

I suppose it must have been just after nine o'clock when the fight was over. Harvey was given the winner on points. His hand was lifted up, and there were cheers for him and for the loser, and then Harvey went over to say a few consoling words to Stan. But Stan was gibbering with rage. He obviously did not agree with the decision; and before anyone could stop him, he had clouted Harvey an almighty wallop on the side of the head with his open glove. Harvey at once hit back; and the fight had started up all over again. The seconds and the referee tried to part them but it was no use. They were determined to see it out. Before long, the opposing seconds were fighting and the little referee had received a wicked punch in the stomach and was lying flat out on his back in the ring. It was good old Harry Knight who came to the rescue then. He quickly lowered the groaning safety curtain.

I tried to slip out of the gallery for I had had enough. But I was caught in that angry crowd. For what had happened on the stage was now being repeated on the floor of the house. Men were standing and jumping on the seats, and fights were taking place downstairs and in the balcony. It was terribly frightening. Those who could do so, managed to get out, but the aisles were jammed as the fighting went on. I saw lots of men struggling on the floor, two others laying about them with walking sticks, collars and ties ripped off, fists flashing on all sides. Nobody knew what was going on behind the safety curtain, but Harry Knight told me afterwards that both boxers collapsed out of sheer fatigue.

At last I managed to get downstairs, worming my way through the press to one of the exits. Then someone turned the gas lights out. But I had got out into the fresh air, leaving the riot behind me, a pitched medieval battle between all Drybrook and half Cinderford. I made my sad and shaken way home. I comforted myself though with the thought that Harvey had won. And then I remembered with a shock that old Harry Knight had not had his pint of bitter. I nearly decided to go back and get it for him but I had had enough of the Empire for one evening.

I learned afterwards that it had all cooled down by ten o'clock, that several men had to appear in court charged with disturbing the peace, and that Harvey and Stan had decided to fight it all out again. I had a lot to tell Edgar when I met him at church next day. Oh, it was a seven days' wonder in our town.

Mother was waiting up for me. She gave me a rather stern glance as I wandered in, and then said, "You'd better eat your bread and cheese and get off to bed. You must be hungry after that long meeting."

I have never met Harvey Blanch from that day to this but I know he is still living. I often wonder if he remembers that boxing match all those years ago, and if he beat Stan Phillips when they fought for the third time.

4 A SEASON OF PLAYS

I SUPPOSE I was about sixteen when I saw my first Shakespeare play. It was *Twelfth Night*. But I had to go fourteen miles into Gloucester to see it, for there was no theatre nearer to my home. It was the Benson Company which performed the play, and I was completely carried away by the poetry of it all. I came out into Westgate Street with my head in the clouds, and continued to mouth some of the more memorable lines for days afterwards, much to the consternation of my patient mother who looked very suspiciously at me from time to time. Though I am always glad I saw the great Sir Frank Benson, I was most struck by the young actress who played the part of Olivia. I cannot remember what her name was, but she bewitched me all right, and I have been a bit in love with her ever since. If she is still living, she will be in her sixties, I think.

But although there was no permanent theatre in my little town, we had our travelling players—barnstormers of the old-time style; I often went to see what they had to offer. They appeared on the scene in early autumn, at the same time as pig-killing and apple-picking. For a week or so beforehand, bills appeared on all the hoardings and in some of the shop windows. You could also come across them stuck on posts and barns, often at drunken angles, in the countryside outside the town. But, wherever they were, they announced to one and all that Mr. Ebley's theatre would, as in previous years, be giving a season of plays, old and new in the Market Yard.

Now this yard must have been the smallest patch of ground on which a theatre ever appeared. It was no more than an apron stage of Forest of Dean mud. But it had the advantage of being in the centre of what was, in those Edwardian days, a grey, drab, mining town, with most of us living on the edge of poverty. The Market yard was next to the Market itself, a squat, corrugated-iron building, where Mrs. Jordan, in spotless white apron, sold the best faggots and peas for miles around, and Johnny Gough, the best cough sweets.

It was amazing what could be assembled on the Market yard. I have seen a complete fair with a roundabout, helter-skelter, cake-walk, rifle range, coconut shy, boxing booth, hoop-la and a medicine man and a cheap-jack into the bargain. The immortal spot acted as a magnet to the youth of the town. I frittered away many a penny on its innocent pleasures, at a time when pennies were not easily come by.

Mr. Ebley's travelling theatre was a wooden structure. One day the yard would be empty; the next, would see a few men at work on the sloping roof; by the evening, the long, rect-angular building would be up, with the seats in position, a cur-tained stage at one end, and a box-office at the other. At eight o'clock sharp on the following Saturday night, with a few late tradesmen still calling their wares, and the incandescent lamps burning brightly, the doors would be opened, and the town would stream in. From then onwards until the end of the winter, there would be one performance nightly except on

Saturdays, when there would be a matinee and two nightly performances.

Ebley's Theatre belongs to the days before the Great War, so I cannot remember with any certainty the names of all the players in his company, though their faces are plain enough to me, even at this distance in time. I only ever succeeded in persuading my mother to allow me to go to one evening performance, but I was a fairly regular attender on Saturday afternoons. That was before the cinema came to seduce us. But I do recall old man Ebley clearly enough, and one or two members of his family. It was he who produced all the plays, acted as stage manager and publicity agent, as well as taking the parts of Napoleon, Sweeney Todd, Maria Marten's father and the Duke of Buckingham. Once I met him, out of character, in the town; to my enormous surprise he turned out to be a thick-set little man with a shock of white hair, wearing a rather stained suit. The dark-eyed, witch-like creature who took our money at the box-office was Mrs. Ebley, I fancy. She had charge of the finances and was also mistress of the company's wardrobe. She played the piano or sang, when music was demanded, and appeared before the footlights as the Empress Josephine, Little Willie's mother in *East Lynne*, Maria Marten's mother, and the Duchess of Buckingham. There was an elder daughter, known locally as "Sweet Nell of Old Drury", who brought tears to the eyes of ladies in the audience with her Maria Marten, and her fallen woman act in *Ten Nights in a Bar Room* or *Father Come Home*. By nature, she was a haughty young woman, I believe, whose flashing, gipsy looks completely hypnotised the young men of the district who flocked to see her whenever she appeared in any part which demanded the minimum of clothing. But she would have none of them. A younger daughter, a minx of about thirteen, who suddenly turned up at school one day, having been chased there by the attendance officer was, for all her maturity, a rather poor scholar when it came to reading and writing. But she regularly brought the house down with her Little Eva in *Uncle Tom's Cabin*. There was also a young man who belonged to the theatre, but I do not think he was an Ebley. It was believed that he was courting the proud-faced daughter, though with little more success than the local boys. He was a pale, pathetic-looking individual with cow-like eyes, whose greatest performance was the dying William in *East Lynne*. He also fancied himself as the public hangman when William Corder was sent to his doom.

This, as far as I remember, was the complete set-up but, by doubling, and even trebling, the parts, they managed, between them, to present a whole season of plays. They must have had about two dozen or so in their repertoire, several of them with the books by old man Ebley himself. It was not uncommon for Napoleon to appear later on in the same play as Wellington's aide-de-camp, or for Charles II to come on, when not needed in that regal capacity, as Nell Gwyn's poor old father. There were occasions when the night's offering demanded an even larger cast than the Ebley Theatre could manage; then a few of the local inhabitants would be enlisted. But more of this later.

In addition to the plays already mentioned, there were such attractions as *Puss in Boots*, *Aladdin*, *Sinbad*, and *The Christmas Fairy*, for the children. These were not pantomimes, but straightforward presentations of the old stories. Occasionally Ebley advertised—for adults only—that his company was going to perform such pieces as *Alone in London*, or *Betrayed*, or *The Secrets of the Monastery*. On these occasions there would be packed houses.

From all accounts, though, the most popular presentations were *East Lynne* and *Uncle Tom's Cabin*. When these were presented, the women of the town would be present in large weeping numbers. And on these occasions it was common for some member of the audience to stand up in her seat and warn Maria that her lover, William Corder, was a villain. Similarly,

the Demon Barber was denied legal parenthood before he had
even begun to lather an intended victim. Of course, Napoleon
was regularly hissed and the Duke of Wellington as regularly
cheered. Certainly on Saturday afternoons we children were
spellbound. We were never surprised that cats could talk, or
that Sinbad was carried on the back of a big bird, high above
our heads, from one side of the stage to the other. The costumes, the words, and the whole atmosphere, gripped us. We
clutched our neighbours tightly when it appeared that the
hero's hopes were going to be dashed to the ground. We
cheered loudly when he triumphed. Some of us got to know the
lines of the plays so well that we used to prompt the actors if
they were at all late on their cues. During the intervals we
regaled ourselves on popcorn and tiger nuts. We munched
chestnuts, gathered from our local trees, littering the floor with
shells and skins. In the time of colds, the smell of eucalyptus
and freshly-peeled oranges intermingled. Sometimes Mr. Ebley
appeared on the stage at the end of a performance in black coat
and tails, having hastily discarded Sinbad's or Dick Whitting-
ton's costumes, in order to tell us what we should be seeing
the following Saturday. What generous measure his little
company gave us. As a matter of fact, I realise now that old
man Ebley was quite an actor and had something more to him
than the exaggerated speech and attitudes of the period.

Then, one Saturday night, my brother took me to see a performance of *The Gunpowder Plot*. I suppose mother had con-
sented, believing innocently that it would improve my knowledge of history. The cast had been enlarged by the inclusion of
some volunteers from the town who fancied themselves as
actors. One of these, Charlie Edwards, was given the part of
the Captain of the Guard; another, Victor Munday, was
Robert Catesby's servant. Now all that the Captain of the
Guard had to say was, "Come, let us search the vaults"; and
all that Robert Catesby's servant had to say was, "Beware of
eavesdroppers." The first act showed the assembled plotters in

Catesby's house deciding how they could get rid of the King and his Parliament. Victor had merely to hand round glasses of wine (cold tea, in fact), put some logs on the fire, and, at the appropriate moment, interrupt the proceedings with the line that he had been repeating to himself since daybreak, "Beware of eavesdroppers." But poor old Victor lost his head. He had soon completed his menial tasks and had got himself so interested in the plot that he decided to give advice. He was heard to mutter, "Ay, I'd do that if I were you," and, "You watch him. He's crafty." So involved did he become that, in spite of the nudges and angry looks of his fellow players, the moment passed for him to deliver his speech. The scene was about to end without it when Victor stepped to the front of the stage, put his hand to his mouth, bent down, and informed the audience in the kind of whisper which could have been heard all over the house, to "Beware of eavesdroppers." It was so funny that people were overcome and rolled out of their seats into the aisles. Victor didn't live the phrase down for years.

The next act was straightforward enough. This consisted of a scene in King James's Palace, followed by another in the chamber of the Houses of Parliament. But there was more trouble in the third act. Charles Edwards not only ordered his five companions (easily recognisable as boys who had just left the grammar school) to "search the vaults", but also led them off the stage to continue the search for Guy in the auditorium. What is more, Edgar White, who was our Sunday School superintendent and was in the audience that evening, joined in the search with them until somebody called out, "Sit down, you silly old fool." Eventually the guard appeared on the stage again, as suddenly disappeared from view to the left, and then returned to the right, dragging Guy Fawkes with them. This unfortunate had already been savaged off stage, his costume sadly disarranged, his wig and beard awry. It was obvious that he was terrified out of his wits, the more especially as Charlie, who worked for one of our butchers, had brought along a steak knife and was threatening to cut his bloody throat if he didn't confess. It was only when James I walked quickly on that the innocent victim was released from his tormentor. Even then, they couldn't get the protesting Charlie off until they had brought the curtain down.

We may not have added to our knowledge of history, but it was a grand, uproarious evening. There were some, of course, who maintained that the whole thing was a hoax. Edgar White said that Charlie and Victor were the best of the lot.

And so the season would come to an end. There would be a last night, with a double bill, for the benefit of one of the members of the company. Parting presents would be handed up from the floor. Mr. Ebley would make a farewell speech. Then the wicker travelling baskets would be packed, the wooden theatre come down and the players disappear almost as quietly as they had come. Although the mud in the Market yard had dried out to fine dust, buxom Mrs. Jordan was still ladling out faggots and peas to contented diners, and generous Johnny Gough still shouting himself hoarse selling his cough drops. The spring had come again. The larks of Gloucestershire were high in the heavens, inviting us to the fields and the freedom of the woods. The Ebleys no doubt, were "resting". But they would be back the following October with all the old favourites and some new pieces obtained, it would be certain, for our special benefit, at enormous expense.

C

5 THE WEDDING

ONE Saturday night I was sitting in the taproom of *The Mount Pleasant* drinking cider with "the boys". The cider was local stuff, called "Stun 'Em", hard and fiery, enough to knock a grown man out after a few mugs of it, let alone a boy still in his 'teens. "The boys" were Bob Whitehouse and Claude Evans. We were all still at school, and ought to have been doing our homework. I suppose we all were in a manner of speaking though it was over the long oak table of our snug little pub. It was a frosty night a few weeks before Christmas. We did not find it easy to turn from the fire and cosiness of that room to the darkness outside and the walk back home on iron roads. But mothers were waiting for us and it was they who had decided that 10 o'clock was our zero hour.

We were just about to leave, when Philip Bustard, the landlord, took me on one side. "Bent you the church organist?"

"Deputy," I apologised.

"That's a pity," he said, "I wanted you to do a job for me."

"What kind of a job?" I asked.

"A wedding," came the solemn answer. "Our Glad's going to marry Percy."

"What, your Glad?" The words slipped out before I knew what I was saying. "Well, I'll have to ask Charlie Walding if I can do the job," I warned him.

"How much?" went on Philip.

"Three half-crowns," I replied, "and a bob for the blower. And I don't know if I can get *him* yet."

We parted happily. I had received my first professional engagement as a musician. I did not doubt it would be all right by the organist. After all, I took some of the children's services for him. I told the boys on the way home and we sorted it all out.

"I'll blow for you," volunteered Bob.

"And I'll turn over the music," chuckled Claude.

"Our Glad" was Gladys, the landlord's only daughter. He was a widower and she was a favourite with everybody. She was very tall, with massive hands like a ribbed leaf in autumn. She wore clothes which hung on her broad frame like curtains, and mammoth shoes, size 9. Her face was red, broad and welcoming, and Shakespeare would have loved it. But Gladys was good-humoured and happy-go-lucky for all her startling appearance, and as earthy as some warm animal of the fields. And she was forty if she was a day.

Percy, on the other hand, was fifteen years her junior and about three-quarters her size. He was the potman at *The Mount Pleasant*. I remember him moving about the pub in a white apron and carrying a tray of glasses, quiet-voiced, neat in all he did, with a rather resigned face, and cheeks as pink as a newly-boiled prawn. He was generally called Perce. "Perce," we shouted, "the same again." "Coming, sir," he would gaily answer.

"Perce," shouted someone else from another corner of the room. "There's a fly in this bitter."

"All right, sir, I'll come and drown it."

Perce had gone bald prematurely and only a few dark, shining hairs remained to be plastered down on his dome to give the faintest suggestion of a parting. We boys used to pull his leg about it. "It's like heaven, Perce. There's no parting there." He was an orphan who, born in mid-Wales, had wandered over the border, and from one job to another, until he had turned up at *The Mount Pleasant* where he had remained ever since. He had long been one of the family and did all the odd jobs about the place, but we had never thought of Glad and Perce as man and wife. We did not even guess that they had been courting.

Well, Charlie Walding was perfectly willing for me to play at the wedding, and the banns were called on the next three Sundays. Not, I should add, without a few titters and guffaws at morning service. And we all found it difficult to associate "Gladys Alberta Bustard" with "Our Glad", and "Percival Seymour Pretoria Griffiths" with "Perce", both of this parish.

The wedding was to take place on the Saturday before Christmas Day. I saw little of both of them in the meanwhile. One evening when we were in *The Mount Pleasant* they weren't there. "They went off to Gloucester for the day," said Philip. "She's gone to be fitted." I met Percy once in the street. He grinned rather sheepishly at me and offered an interesting comment on the weather, that it was not bad for the time of the year.

The great day arrived. The wedding had been timed for 12.30. I told mother I should be back home by half-past one at the latest, so she said she would keep dinner for me. When I got to the church, with plenty of time to spare, it had, to my surprise, already begun to fill. I spotted a number of folk there who were far more regular customers of *The Mount Pleasant* than attenders at St. Stephen's Church. By twenty past, most of the pews had been taken by a noisy, ill-assorted crowd, who lolled in their seats, turned round, chatted to friends, and generally made themselves a nuisance. On several occasions the verger had to tell them to keep quiet and to remember where they were. It quite upset me. As a matter of fact, from the moment I put my foot in the church that day everything went wrong for me. To begin with, I could not find my surplice. I had forgotten that it had gone to be washed for Christmas Day. Eventually I found an old one of the curate's, but he was six inches taller than me. The blessed thing stretched almost to the ground and I nearly broke my neck when I was making my way to the organ. Then when I got there it kept getting in between my feet and the pedals. In the end I had to tuck it into my trousers. Then to my horror, I discovered the blower hadn't turned up. Bob had let me down, then. As time was getting on, I couldn't wait any longer for him. So I glanced round the congregation to see if I could spot a likely conscript. My search was not very rewarding. It looked as if I should have to make a choice between "Silly" Ted, who might at any moment stop blowing, and go for a short walk ("To cool me 'ands, mister," he once told me), and Billy Whiffin, who had once been the official blower, and was now over eighty. I just couldn't ask *him*, in case he dropped dead from exhaustion in the middle of the Wedding March. I was just about to gamble on Ted when Bob came rushing in, panting and red-faced. He slipped behind the organ gasping out apologies. "Sorry. Been cleaning my bike. Thought it was half-past twelve."

"It was," I hissed at him, "and it's that now."

I started to play the first voluntary, a sickly piece by a minor nineteenth century German composer. At least it served to quieten the mob. Before it came to an end on a soft diapason, the vicar had banged into the vestry and was robing. I peeped over the top of the organ lift. The bridegroom had not arrived. Neither had he appeared by a quarter to one. A terrible fear came over me that Perce had jilted her at the last minute. By ten to one I had played three of my repertoire of four pieces and only had Mendelssohn's Wedding March left. (This in a simpli-fied version.) And I couldn't give them that *yet*. So I began to regale them with a series of hymns, each ornamented with my best twiddly bits. I don't know what they made of *Lo, He comes with Clouds Descending* followed by *Glorious Things of Thee are spoken*. The imp in me wanted to play *Fierce Raged the Tempest O'er the Deep* but I restrained myself in time. The Vicar was fidgeting by the vestry door; I knew he would soon be in a vile temper.

Then when I was enjoying myself, improving on *The Voice That Breathed O'er Eden*, Perce and his best man walked in, rather unsteadily, I thought, up the central aisle. I wondered if they had been fortifying themselves. Perce had a glazed look and did not seem to be with us. But who, in the name of fortune, had told him to wear plus fours and brown patent leather shoes? I could hear laughter gently ripping around the church. I went on playing. Bob whispered from the back of the organ, " 'Ere, go easy, I'm puffed." But I just had to go on, hymns, variations, everything I knew except, of course, the Wedding March. I could see Perce just below me sitting bolt upright in his pew. Then, at twenty-five past one, when several of the congregation had already left, there was a flutter at the bottom of the church, and everybody rose, that is, all but "Silly" Ted. Unfortunately, I lost my head and started to play the Wedding March as Gladys entered on her father's arm. Hot with confusion, I watched them, out of the corner of my eye, moving very slowly up the church. Philip was wearing a loud check suit, with a fancy spotted waistcoat, an enormous yellow cravat—and spats. His bowler hat was clutched tightly to his paunch. He looked like an old-fashioned bookie going to a party. But as long as I live I shall never forget the sight of Gladys. She was a symphony in purple. And it was a purple of so violent a hue that she could have passed for a comic Roman empress in fancy dress. Her frock was purple, her shoes were purple, her veil was purple, her purple toque was embellished with knots of artificial Parma violets. She carried a bunch of pink carnations. As they got nearer, it became obvious to me that *they* had fortified themselves, too. Not that they were unsteady. Only splendid and glorious. Gladys was a great purple ship in full sail. She and her smiling father walked up to the waiting Vicar who was looking as black as thunder. There were no bridesmaids. Someone pushed Perce into his proper place where he stood, spellbound, and in utter dejection, But, bless me, when Gladys and her father had got as far as the choir steps, they did not stop there, but turned, in grandeur, down the north aisle. The congregation were still standing. Even "Silly" Ted had got on a seat and was peering over the tops of shoulders. I went on playing with every stop out. Gladys and her father got to the bottom of the church. Now, I thought, it will all come right. But, dear me, no. They then made for the south aisle and paraded up that. By the time the ridiculous perambulations had finished, they had been right round the church. But at last they were by Percy's side and the service began. I was sweating like a pig.

Then Percy suddenly began hiccuping. The best man could not find the ring and had to fumble in all his pockets for it. When at last he discovered it, he further enlivened the proceedings by turning round, holding it on high and saying, "I got 'un. I knew I had 'un somewhere." When asked if she would take Percy to be her lawful wedded husband, Gladys convulsed us by saying, "Of course." "Just say 'I will'," barked the Vicar. Percy went on hiccuping.

Somehow or other they got to the end of it. I cannot remember all the details. But the Vicar preached no sermon and did not appear again. As they were going into the vestry to sign the register, a christening party turned up at the bottom of the church and sat in the seats near the font. And when I struck up the Wedding March again, the baby went into competition with me. Perce, hanging on his wife's arm, looked more miserable than ever. As they walked past the baby Percy gave it a very old-fashioned look.

They got away in the end, though. But the best man forgot

to pay me and I had to go round to the pub that evening to pick up my three half-crowns and the bob for the blower. And I wanted to ask Philip where the bride and bridegroom were spending their honeymoon. I soon found out. *The Mount Pleasant* was packed from cellar to ceiling and the cider and the beer were flowing. Gladys, still magnificent in her wedding purple, was serving with Percy behind the bar. He had perked up a bit. But she was so overwhelmingly happy that, in her joy, she was slopping the beer all over the place, knocking over the glasses with her great be-ringed hands, blowing kisses to one and all—the first lady of *The Mount Pleasant*. And Philip was the potman that night.

6 SATURDAY NIGHT

SATURDAY night was "gang" night, the more the merrier, the noisier the better, with the whole town at our disposal.

I think that Saturday nights in autumn meant most of all to me. They were rarely ever planned in any detail but, at about five o'clock, I would find myself sitting down to a crumpet and celery tea with my second-best suit on and the gaudiest flower in my buttonhole. My hair would be plastered down and shining like the full moon, with a far too lavish dressing of Harry Dobbs's "Kozo". Harry was our local barber and "Kozo", which he sold to the youth of the town at sixpence a box, was, according to the elegant lettering on its lid, "Compounded of the finest ingredients procurable and containing a rare and exotic Eastern perfume." Unbelievers were of the opinion, however, that Harry's pomade was made of cartgrease, coconut oil and a dash of verbena. The smell of that coconut oil lingers with me now. The suit was, as were the suits of all my companions, of the best navy-blue serge, bought, if I remember correctly, for about twenty-five shillings, and continually fighting a losing battle against shiny seat and complete shapelessness. The trousers, having been pressed between the mattresses of my bed since the previous Sunday morning, had creases so sharp that rude grownups were prone to caution me "not to cut my fingers on them". But it was the shoes which added the final lustre to the getup.

Polished until I could see my distorted face in their toecaps, they were made of a fancy leather, whose colour was a cross between the under-belly of a frog and the skin of an over-ripe apple. Arrayed in my young man's glory, and smelling so strongly that my mother kept her safe distance from me, I would finish tea and then enter upon a mode of behaviour which suggested that I was in the early stages of St. Vitus's Dance. Sooner or later, mother, who would be washing up the tea things, sparing my navy-blue and adolescent dignity at the same time, would call to me from the scullery. "And where do you think *you* are going in that getup tonight?" Scarcely pausing in my fidgeting by the window, I usually gave her the same answer. "O, nowhere in particular—just down town with the boys." What bravado! Just "down town", as if I were going up West in order to call at my club and later take dinner with the quality at a fashionable restaurant. "Town" consisted of one main street and four side ones and a population of about three thousand. But the point was that it was *my* town, the only one I knew, apart from the bewildering city of Gloucester.

My window-gazing would be rewarded eventually by the sight of one of the "boys" coming to call for me. Now, it didn't matter whether it was Sam Roberts, Alfie Jenkins or Les Evans, each would be dressed in much the same way as I. Of course, there would be minor differences of taste and fashion, a more dazzling tie, or socks whose hue bore little relationship to the general colour scheme, but there would always be the navy-blue suit, the buttonhole, the handkerchief in the breast pocket, and, when the caller got nearer, the inevitable "Kozo". Within the next few minutes there would be other callers.

Of course, none of them ever knocked at the door. They just walked in, greeted my mother, and then, as if they did not know the answer already, hailed me with, "Coming out tonight?"

Eventually, the little blue-serged company would move off "down town", well washed and chattering, and taking up the whole of the road, as if its members were the only inheritors of the Kingdom of Heaven on earth. We would be oblivious to the remarks of those old ladies and gentlemen who were leaning over their gates, or pottering round their front gardens, and would saunter, with hands in pockets, and rattling our coppers and few bits of silver, down the hill, past the church until we got to the cinema. We moved silently past Miss Emily Smith's house because, on a number of occasions, with trowel in hand and fantastic straw hat on her head, she had been heard to mutter under her breath, as we strolled into her view, the single and highly inaccurate word, "Louts".

We always spent a short time looking at the stills outside the cinema. In those days seats were ridiculously cheap and, even at our advanced age, we could get in for the sum of fourpence. But the programme had to be very attractive in order to tempt us to enter. We always had the greatest difficulty in preventing Alfie Jenkins from leaving the ranks in order to ride with Tom Mix over the Western plains; Sam Roberts, a great barrel of a boy, took some stopping when Lon Chaney was on; Les Evans was all for Charlie Chaplin; and I must admit that I felt the strongest pull on both my heart, and my purse-strings, when Nazimova was prepared to weep and die for me.

Perhaps it was the magical sound of her name which was the great attraction for me. Nazimova—and I was stepping in her snowy tracks across the wild, wild wastes of Russia and following her to the gates of Moscow itself. However we rarely broke our ranks. With a pert word or two to pigtailed Margery Banks, earning her five-and-sixpence a week in the paybox, who, being about our own age, gave back better than she got, we left the cinema with its clicking machine and smell of celluloid behind us, and strolled into the shopping centre. Not that we had come there to shop or even to look in the windows. In any case, only the bike shop had any interest for us. We merely walked to the bottom of the main street on one side, and then up to the top of it on the other. In so doing we would hear Tom Mason, the butcher, trying to convince would-be customers that his beef that week was as tender as a woman's heart, Billy Bonser, the greengrocer, offering oranges at forty a shilling and ripe bananas at a half-penny each, and Herbie Barter, that his very dead codfish were "all alive-o". As we proceeded on our evening parade it was customary to greet one's contemporaries, to touch our greasy forelocks and to blush like beetroots if we saw the Vicar or "The Gaffer", our schoolmaster, and to whistle or to make various clucking noises if our eyes happened to light on some of the more attractive members of the other sex. Occasionally, these young ladies would return our overtures, but they were rarely so compelling as to cause any of us to desert. There was one occasion, however, when Les Evans' heart failed him and, with a guilty "Shan't be long, chaps," followed, or I should say, stalked, a trim little figure down the main street, over the railway crossing and, eventually, out of our gaze. We did not see Les any more that night but, on the following morning at church, we enquired tactfully how his affair had prospered. He looked at us with sad and perplexed eyes and said, "It were her mother." We learned afterwards that Les had pursued the "trim little figure" four miles out into the country before he had seen her face and discovered the sobering truth.

Now all this may seem innocent and unexciting. It was certainly innocent except for that unfortunate lapse by Les Evans. But it was never unexciting. In our blue-suited peram-bulations we felt ourselves to be the kings of the earth, celestial cockey-walkers, the pride and glory of the town. We saw everything and everyone and we believed that everyone saw us. We never knew when a horse and cart was going to run away, a motor-car break down, the town band bray its brassy nocturne on the autumn air, or, if our luck happened to be in, a grandstand view of a fight outside *The King's Head*.

Having glutted ourselves with all that the main street had to offer, we now explored the side streets in turn. In one of these there was always the possibility of seeing a cheapjack offering his assorted wares beneath the hissing naphtha flares, and again we would have to lay violent hands on Alfie Jenkins in order to stop him spending his money on a solid gold watch or on one of the new-fangled safety razors. ("But I shall need it sometime, shan't I?") We viewed Sam Roberts with some disapproval when he once bought for "Only a bob, ladies and gentlemen" a very ornate bottle containing about a pint of Californian Poppy scent. We wondered as to its destination but the mystery was solved on the following day when, raucous-voiced tenors and basses of the church choir, we passed Mrs. Roberts as we processed down the aisle singing the last hymn. Have I made it up, or did it really happen, that, as we drew near to her pew, we were bellowing "What though the spicy breezes blow soft o'er Ceylon's isle?" Having circum-navigated that round space in one of the side streets known as "The Triangle", and if there was nothing else to see or do, after all that we had been seeing and doing that evening, we began to think very seriously about eating. I do not think we ever gave a name to this intended meal for there would be one called "supper" waiting for us when we returned to our homes. It was just that we were boys, were hungry, and had money in our pockets. It was at this stage that we gave further proof of the democratic nature of our basic ethics. We told each other exactly how much money we had and took it for granted that we could share in the common pool. There was a far worse problem to solve. It was a problem which confronted us every Saturday night. What should we eat and where should we go to eat it? Considering the unambitious circumstances in which we and the town were placed, there was an astonishing range of choice and luscious menus available for our enjoyment. You could have fish and chips at "Fishy" Lewis's, faggots and peas at Mrs. Jordan's stall in the market place, brawn sandwiches and a drink known to the management as coffee, but to us by a ruder name, at Woodman's, or, if still remembering the dignity of our suits, a plate of cold meat and pickles at what we called "The Caff", and others "The Café", but whatever our final decision, we were certain of a good blow-out and the glittering prospect that we should still have some money left. If none of these select foods satisfied, we could always fall back on our own domestic and culinary skill by streaming into Richard Westaway's grocery shop and buying tins of salmon and condensed milk. Once, with a daring beyond our years, we also bought a bottle of Tarragona Wine, sold to us by Alfie Jenkins' brother who worked in the shop, at the fabulous price of 2s. 3d. Then, with the tins in our pockets and the bottle safely under one of our coats, we would leave the shop and, as bold as brass, walk across "The Triangle", into the main street and make our way like desperadoes into the woods which circled the town. The first thing we did, when we had found a secret enough spot, was to make a bonfire and then, forgetful of our suits, to sit round it and regale ourselves on the alternate consumption of pink salmon, eaten with a pocket knife, and condensed milk straight from the punctured tin. Never, at any time, did we need corkscrews and tin-openers. I have no doubt that there were occasions when Alfie burnt a hole in his trousers, when I cut my fingers, when "Kozo" ran in streams down Sam's face, but I cannot remember a single occasion when any of us were ever sick. Further, I have some recollection of one Saturday night when we added half-cooked pigs' trotters to the feast.

But Saturday night was drawing near to Sunday morning. Reassembling our gorged ranks, we would leave the woods to the owls and the fading light and make for the town again. As we slowly made our way up the long hill and back to our homes, we said very little to each other. There was nothing to say. We had said it all, or had it been all said for us? And, in any case, we should be all together again the next day. But that was Sunday. That would be different. This was Saturday night.

7 BRASS BAND

THERE has always been a brass band in our town. For as long as I can remember it has solemnly saluted the happy morn at Christmas, given any number of open air concerts in summer, and paraded through our rather drab streets at all seasons of the year. Our band, in vivid blue and gold uniform, was one of the more familiar and stirring sights of my childhood.

At strength, our band numbered thirty players, most of them miners, though as few as a dozen were sometimes seen in attendance at local Sunday School Treats. And though there were thirty names on the books, there were only twenty-six instruments available, some shimmering with much loving care and polish, others battered and dull.

The youngest member of the band, Roy Barnard, was, at thirteen, already an accomplished cornetist; a great future was prophesied for him in the larger musical world. Nobody played runs and trills better than Roy. What is more, he knew it, and never let the rest of us forget it. The oldest member of our band, Charlie Teague, weighed sixteen stone, and for forty of his sixty-five years, carried the big drum and whacked it vigorously for generations of delighted children. To my regret, I was never a member of the band myself, because I had too much homework to do and couldn't spare the time to go to the practices in the band room at *The Globe Inn*.

We were a district of brass bands. There were almost as many within ten miles of our town as there are French cheeses or wines in a countryside of similar size. These bands were either brass, or silver, according to their status and how they had fared in band contests. Once or twice a year our local bands competed in a contest to decide which was the champion band. And for this great occasion there would be famous judges, from outside the district, and handsome money prizes. There was also a great deal of laying of bets on the side. In fact, rivalry was so keen that some of the bands had been known to engage professional conductors to coach them up to standard. The repertoires of all the bands consisted of little more than selections from operas and oratorios, popular marches and waltzes, and simple arrangements of national songs. Though the music was not, perhaps, very adventuring, the playing was hearty enough. And everybody enjoyed themselves.

One year, just before the first World War, our band won everlasting glory. It decided to compete in the National Brass Band Championships at the Crystal Palace, largely, I suspect, because of the excitement of a journey to London and back, and all expenses paid. It is true most of us were surprised when it was placed first in its class and came back home in triumph to march about the town with Roy Barnard, all smiles and blowing his head off, and Charlie Teague treating his drum as if it had been an enemy for years. And the band had won enough prize money to change over from brass to silver instruments, and to new uniforms, for about half the players. The town had not known anything like it for years. From then

D

onwards the band styled itself the Silver Prize Band, though it was rather amusing to hear Charlie Teague's wife saying, round about this time, "Ever since our Charlie came back from London he's been as bold as brass."

But I was a member of our local male voice choir. We sang such contemporary masterpieces as *Martyrs in the Arena* and *The Pirates' Song*. We were a pretty good lot, on the whole, I believe, though some of our tenors were inclined to sing out of tune, and only four of the basses could read music properly. One year—I suppose I was in my early twenties—our conductor, Harry Dobbs, entered us for the male voice choir competition which was to be part of the annual Brass Band Festival to be held in Lydney Park (by kind permission of Lord Bledisloe, P.C., G.C.M.G., K.B.E.), about nine or ten miles from my home. The festival was to take place on August Bank Holiday. That put a few of us in a dilemma, for August Bank Holiday was the day when the Baptist Chapel always had its mammoth treat. This was as fixed in the town's calendar as any of the laws of England. I do not believe they would have *had* a treat if there had not been an August Bank Holiday. Now, although many of us were not Baptists by conviction, we generally found ourselves, as did every other denomination, with our girl friends, at their treat. But after a lot of discussion, we decided to give the treat a miss that year and all go over to Lydney to sing for the honour of the town. We might even catch a glimpse of his lordship. Very few of us had ever seen a real live lord.

At our last rehearsal, Harry Dobbs impressed on us that we had to be outside *The Globe* at twelve-thirty sharp on the Bank Holiday, for it would take just under the hour to get us to Lydney Park. Of course we went in Bert Prosser's charabanc, the only one, at that time, our town possessed.

As I made my way down the hill to the meeting place I thought I was going to be late for I could see there was already quite a crowd waiting outside the pub. And when I got there

I discovered, to my surprise, that about half of the fellows belonged to the brass band. Soon more of the band came along and more of the choir, all dressed in best suits and wearing trilby hats. Trilby hats were in fashion for such events.

Then the dreadful truth was revealed. There, in front of us, was one charabanc and there, waiting on the pavement, were two bodies of musicians, about sixty in all, planning to go off that afternoon to the festival. There had obviously been a frightful muddle. It came out later that Bert Prosser had not only lost our secretary's letter but had also completely forgotten about it. He pointed out that he had written in his book, "Bank Holiday. Take band to Lydney festival (what a hope!)"

Well, this was a very unfortunate beginning. Some of the men were all for going back home, and then later, to the Baptist treat, but Bert Prosser said he could make the double journey at top speed and still bring us all to Lydney on time. He thought it would be fairest all round if the first load consisted of half the band and half the choir; the rest of us could be taken the second time. But Jim Noble, the conductor of the band, broke in with, "That's no good. We got to be there by two o'clock, for the march past."

I suggested that the whole sixty of us should get into the charabanc and sit on each other's knees, but Bert Prosser said that he would have none of that for he doubted if the vehicle would ever get up the hills or stop when it was going down them. So, after a lot more talk, it was settled that the older choristers and bandsmen should travel in the charabanc, and the younger ones whizz over to Lydney on their bikes. "But, mind you," pointed out Jim Noble, "you've got to be at Lydney Cross by five to two at the latest." And "Mind you," emphasised Harry Dobbs, "it's no good any of you turning up later than two thirty. And don't forget your music." The set piece for the male voice choir contest that year was *The Hallelujah Chorus* from *Messiah*.

As I was one of the younger ones I was supposed to go over on my bike. But I hadn't got a bike. I had kept quiet while all the argument was going on. Luckily, Harold Davis, who played the euphonium in the band, had a motor bike, and offered to take me on his pillion.

Well, we watched Bert Prosser drive off with the old men, and then we younger ones made off to find our own transport. Harold turned out to be rather a terrifying driver so that I was more than thankful when, after we had been ripping along for about ten minutes, Harold suddenly stopped, turned round, and said, "I've left my euphonium behind. I know I brought it down to *The Globe*. But I took it back home when we went to get the bike." There was nothing for it. We had to turn round and go back to get Harold's instrument. Now came the problem of how to carry the thing on a motor bike. Clearly Harold couldn't do it. So I had to, and very uncomfortable and inconvenient it was. I hung nervously on to him with one arm and carried his euphonium under the other.

But our troubles were not yet over. Just after we got to the *Speech House Hotel* the bike spluttered and stopped. "No petrol," muttered Harold. "But I thought you said you had a gallon," I replied. "Well, so did I," went on Harold. "My Dad must have used the bike to go to work yesterday." Fortunately they sold petrol at the hotel and when we had filled up, Harold suggested that we should go inside and have a drink to calm our nerves. We had almost finished our second glass of cider when we saw, through the tap room window, Bert Prosser's charabanc chugging by. We rushed out and waved to them. Some of them waved back and Harry Dobbs called out, "You get a move on. You're going to be late." So off we went through the heart of the Forest of Dean, along the cool, tree-shaded summer roads, arriving, with half-an-hour to spare, at Lydney Cross.

As I was getting off the bike I realised I had left Harold's euphonium behind me. I remembered putting it on the table of the tap room but we had not gone back into the hotel when the charabanc came along. Harold was downcast. I felt dreadful. "Well," said Harold, "there is just time to go back to the *Speech House* and get it." But a worse catastrophe was to follow.

When we got back to the hotel the euphonium was not there. The landlord had not even seen it. "I wasn't serving at the time," he told us. "My missus was. And she's gone off to Cinderford to the Baptist Treat." Harold sat down with his face in his hands and stared miserably at the wall. I could have committed suicide. And then I noticed that there, beneath a pair of magnificent deer antlers, was fixed a serpent. I don't mean a snake, either, but the old-fashioned musical instrument. There it was, the whole fantastic eight feet of it. I looked at Harold. "Do you think you could borrow that?" I said. "It would be better than nothing." "Don't be a sillier fool than you've been already," countered Harold, "what's the good of that thing to me?" We left the hotel and dashed back to Lydney. We got there just in time for the march past. And by good fortune Harold was able to borrow a euphonium from a Welsh band which had only entered for the main contest and not for the march past. But Harold was not too pleased, because the instrument was a brass one. He felt that he was letting the band down.

Fourteen bands played in Lydney that August Bank Holiday. When our Silver Prize Band marched past, blazing away at *The Washington Post*, we all cheered. I do not think anybody noticed that Harold was carrying the only brass instrument in his band. His face, though, was not very comforting. And when the bands had marched down the street singly and had been judged for their performance, they all joined together and marched down the street again, as one intermingled brass and silver body, three hundred bandsmen out for the day. I doubt if Lydney had ever heard such a noise before. When the march past was over we all made our way to the Park where we found that all the members of our male voice choir had arrived except two of the tenors. They never did turn up. Nor were they reported as being present at the Baptist Treat. But we could do without both of them for we knew that neither was very certain of his part.

There were crowds of people in the park but as we knew few of the faces we felt like strangers in a strange land. Just when the proceedings were due to begin his lordship arrived and made a welcoming speech from the platform in the centre of the ground. He told us how much he liked music, asked us to respect his park, and then left us, as he had to attend an important meeting. I wondered if he had gone off to the Baptist Treat, too.

We were last in the order of singing. Considering all things, we sang *The Hallelujah Chorus* very well and when the results were given, the professor from Cardiff and the organist from Birmingham had placed us second. They congratulated us on our expression and our enthusiasm, but said that some of our parts were a bit shaky. Not half as shaky as some of us had been feeling, I could have told them.

But the male voice item was not what the crowd had come for. They were waiting for the brass band contest. Our Silver Prize Band had to play first of all. Alas, everything seemed to go wrong for them. One of the music stands fell down and took two more with it. This caused the player of the flugel horn to wobble terribly. Then one of the tenor trombones knocked off the peaked cap of one of the cornets in front of him. Twice the band had to stop and start again. Harold looked very nervous with his brass instrument. Then the worst thing of all happened. The band had almost come to the end of their piece when the conductor's trousers started to come down. He always was a vigorous conductor but, with all that had been going on that afternoon, he had snapped his braces. The crowd roared with laughter as he had to keep changing his baton from hand to hand. Soon the band was overcome with laughter, too, and when the piece was ended they collapsed, almost in hysterics, on the platform. Poor man, he didn't know where to hide himself, so he jumped to the ground and made for one of the tents as best he could.

Everybody expected that our band would be bottom. But at five o'clock when the judges gave the results, we learned that the band, like the choir, had been placed second. The judges said that they had listened to a very moving performance, full of lightness and good humour, with some brilliant euphonium playing. The prize was a shield and £20. But this was not enough to cheer up Harold. He was still worried about his euphonium. "If I had had my own instrument," he said, "we should have been first." "Don't you believe it," answered Charlie Teague. "It was them braces that done it."

On the way back home Harold and I called at the *Speech House*. The landlord's wife had returned from the Baptist Treat. Yes, she said, the trumpet thing was all right. She had put it away safely in her kitchen. "And I've given it a bit of a shine up while you've been away." Harold clasped it to his bosom as if it were his first-born. And then, with a happy smile spreading over his tired face, he solemnly played through the euphonium part of the test piece. The landlord's wife looked on in wonder. "Well," she said. "And did they give you second prize for *that*?"

8 FLOWER SHOW

Our Flower Show always took place on the last Saturday in July, too late, my grandfather said, for the roses, and too early for the apples. But it had to be on *that* Saturday because the Co-op Penny Bank had their gala and turn-out on the following Saturday and the Baptist Chapel their monster treat on the August Bank Holiday.

I grew up with our Flower Show, for, like every other boy in our town I was taken to see it year after year. It was the thing to do. And as my grandfather used to exhibit, it was a family duty to be present. Flowers, fruit and vegetables did not greatly interest us but there were always the stalls, the guessing competitions, and the swings and roundabouts on which we could spend our pennies, so we were never completely bored. And there was always the band to listen to and all our friends to see, and generally some display or other. One year they had a riding display by the crack horsemen of the Royal Gloucestershire Yeomanry but that went on too long and they all lost their tempers. Another time they sent a balloon up with a man in it and he, poor chap, did not come down for sixteen hours—somewhere in the Black Mountains, I believe.

When I was about twenty I was appointed Assistant Secretary of our Flower Show. "Appointed", perhaps, is hardly the word. John Emery, our school master, was the Secretary of the Show that year and I was a very new member of his staff. So it was really a case of my having to do what I was told. Emery thought it would be a good idea if I became Assistant Secretary, so that was that. He told me, with great effect, that it would be good for my career, important people in the town would notice me, the job would give me a sense of authority, and, in any case, I should be able to relieve him of some of the minor details. As he was a man who generally got his own way with everybody he did not find it difficult to convince the Committee that I was the very man for the job.

Preparations for the Show began in January. There was a meeting of the Committee in John Emery's front parlour. Snow was falling outside and I could not help thinking what an act of faith it all was. The chairman was Dr. Bangara, an Indian doctor, and one of the most popular men in the town. But he was far too mild and gentle to be a good chairman. Emery contradicted him most of the time. There were also present Willie Bolton, the newsagent, Richard Westaway, the grocer, Wilkins, who had a sweetshop, and his son, Sam Perkins and Fred Thomas who were miners, and two silent ladies I had never seen before. At that meeting, which went on for nearly four hours, it was decided to advertise the show in the local papers, arrange to have the bills, schedules, programmes and prize tickets printed, order the marquees, and appoint the judges. There was quite a lot of bad feeling let loose about the last two items. Richard Westaway wanted us to get the marquees from a new firm in Newport on the grounds that last year's marquees which had come from Cheltenham were too expensive and, also, that the men who came to put them up were very rude to him when he offered them some advice. Emery, who was Welsh, supported Westaway. Eventually we decided on the Newport firm. The question of judges caused such a stir that the matter had to be adjourned to the next meeting. Apparently all last year's judges had been local men who had awarded the prizes to friends and relatives. Fred Thomas was all for going farther afield. His wife had exhibited in the sweet pea class for ten years and had never yet won a prize—and it was only because of the jealousy of the judge. "Well," chimed in Emery, "if we have new judges from outside the district we shall have to pay for them." "And why not?" snapped Willie Bolton. "We've got plenty of money in the bank." So it went on and on.

By the end of June most of the arrangements had been made. At least we thought so. As Secretary, Emery wrote the letters. As Assistant Secretary, I posted them. For most of the time that summer I was his fetch-and-carry boy. It is true that he did allow me to sort out the show cards one evening and to collect the advertisements for the official programme from the local tradesmen. This was the most thankless task of all for several of the tradesmen were abominably rude to me when they heard what an inch of advertising space was going to cost.

The Friday before the day of the Flower Show arrived. There were no clouds in the sky. The four huge marquees were due to come that afternoon from Newport and to be up by the evening so that the show stands and display tables could be moved in. Matters had been so arranged that there was very little work going on inside the school that afternoon so Emery told me to go down to the Recreation Ground, where the Show was always held, and await the arrival of the marquees. There were a few other members of the Committee waiting, too, and one or two strangers. One of these was the County Bee-keeping expert. He was unpacking a bee tent in which he was going to give an illustrated lecture on Show day. The stalls were going up, too, and the swings and roundabouts, and a huge block of coal, whose weight was to be guessed at, was being carefully lowered from a colliery wagon. The hurdles for the sheep dog trials had already been placed in position at the top end of the field, and the wire cages for the fowls and rabbits were piled up near the gate. But, alas, there were no marquees. As they had not come by four o'clock I raced back up to school to tell Emery. He told me to go back down to the field at once and not to fuss so much. They would be there all right. The Newport firm was very reliable. Emery appeared an hour later, greeting me with, "Where are the marquees, boy?" in the kind of voice intended to make me feel personally responsible for anything which might go wrong. "Well, I'll soon put that right," he muttered and stumped off to telephone to Newport. Half an hour later he marched into the ground again looking as black as thunder. "The fools," he rasped out, "the silly, careless fools. They've muddled the dates. Thought it was next week. But I told them exactly what I thought of them. All their tents are out but they will do their best to get some here by tomorrow morning. The men will be here by five-thirty." And then, with a side-long glance at me, "And you'd better be here when they come."

I hardly slept a wink that night. I was scared of over-sleeping. When I did drop off I had the most fantastic nightmare of hundreds of marquees floating away into the Gloucestershire skies with members of the committee hanging grimly on to the guy ropes. But I was down on the dew-wet Recreation Ground next morning just after five. There was a keen breeze blowing and first smoke going up from some of the cottages. To everybody's relief, the marquees arrived at seven o'clock, and were soon up. They looked a fine sight with their little flags waving bravely at the top. O, it is going to be a splendid day, I thought. I now made my way home to have my breakfast. I met Emery on his way to the ground to survey the scene. "Good morning, boy," he said. "I've had my breakfast. I hear the marquees have arrived. I knew that firm wouldn't let us down. Not after what I told them." He left me speechless with the words, "You know, don't you, that the gates will be opened at 9 o'clock for the exhibitors. Don't be late." It was then nearly half past eight.

That morning there was a constant stream of exhibitors, who came in every kind of transport. The marquees began to fill up. Two were given over to flowers and vegetables, one to fruit, and one to honey, home-made cakes, pickles and jams, needlework, children's wildflower collections and floral arrangements (ladies only). Everybody seemed to be coming or going. The sun was rising higher in the sky. I gave committee men their badges of office, handed out programmes to those who were going to sell them, met exhibitors, and reported progress from time to time to Emery who sat in state at a trestle table in a bell-tent not far from one of the big marquees. Over the entrance to his tent was a hand-written notice which read, "Hon. Sec. No Admittance Except on Business. All Complaints must be accompanied by a fee of 1s. 6d." Emery was also mounting guard over the cups, medals, and prizes, and ticking off the entries in a large red foolscap notebook.

As I dashed here and there for him I could not help thinking that if ever I became Secretary of the Flower Show I should also find the right kind of idiot to act as Assistant Secretary.

Over in one corner of the field a smaller marquee was being painfully raised by a squad consisting of an old, straw-hatted man and two clumsy young men who kept on tripping over the tent pegs. This was soon to be labelled "Refreshments", though most of us knew it as "the tea and beer tent". In another corner, the finishing touches were being put to a pit which had been dug for the roasting of an ox later that evening by a professional ox-roaster from Bristol.

By eleven-thirty, with the flags on top of the marquees barely fluttering, everything was ready for the judging of the exhibits to begin. There were four judges. I first handed them their round red cardboard badges of office and then, headed by John Emery, who had now emerged fresh and businesslike from his tent with a sheaf of papers under his arm, the perambulation began. The first judge, from Ross-on-Wye, was a tall, military-looking man in morning dress. He turned out to be a retired major of the Engineers, well known for his wonderful flower garden and an expert on the growing of soft fruit. Next to him was a small round man, not unlike a prosperous beetle, a famous judge from London, of rabbits, fowls and cage birds. He was wearing a bowler hat and large horn-rimmed glasses. He was followed (so the programme said) by James McWhirter Drummond, head gardener to a titled lady in Worcestershire. I learned afterwards that he had begun life as a gardener's boy at Balmoral. Lean, white-bearded, hawk-eyed, he was an authority on the growing of vegetables and had had a potato named after him, *Drummond's Early*. And the fourth judge was Lady Felicity Wintringham, who was responsible for the home and children's classes. Willie Bolton informed me that she was related to one of the silent ladies on our committee, and had at one time been Head Mistress of a high-class girls' public school. She strode along like a man with the kind of look on her square face which made me fearful of the fate of some of the entries of our local housewives. I brought up the rear. My chief job was to place the prize cards on the winning entries—first, second, third, and highly commended.

The judges worked quickly and efficiently and I could see at once that they knew what they were doing. All the same, there was going to be trouble when some of the exhibitors saw the results. There always was. My grandfather, for instance, would go purple in the face when he learned that his cos lettuce had not even got a Highly Commended. And what Jack Selway, who had always won first prize for Victoria plums would say when he discovered that he had been beaten into second place by Frank Morgan, his rival from Littledean, I dared not imagine. The judges spent most of the time deciding which of the great, powerful-smelling floral displays by the professional seedsmen should be awarded the Silver Medal, the highest award in the Show. As they couldn't agree, they consulted John Emery who suggested that each of the displays should be given a silver medal. "Must think of the future," he chuckled.

The judging over, we strolled across to the Refreshment tent for luncheon—cold Severn salmon and salad, with strawberries and cream to follow, washed down by beer, cider and lemonade. I had to act as an extra waiter but I saw to it that I got my share of everything that was going. Emery spent most of his time chatting to Lady Felicity. We had not quite finished eating and drinking when, in the distance, we heard the rising and falling strains of the approaching bands, heading the long carnival procession which had been parading the town for the past hour.

Soon the procession burst into the ground, the most fantastic of assemblies, followed, in a few moments, by the eager general public, streaming in through the hot, clicking turnstiles. There was another set of judges for the carnival, some oddly-hatted, curiously-dressed, mad-looking ladies who were on holiday at a near-by guest house. I could hear them twittering like doves as their heads came together and they made up their minds. The procession of every character known and unknown to mankind, straggled slowly round the ground with the two silver bands in attendance. Some of the children looked very tired and bedraggled in their costumes for there was little breeze, and they had been on the march for far too long. "But

I like to see children at a Flower Show, don't you?" said one of the lady judges. "They're flowers, too, you know."

And so the day wore on. As anticipated, there were the usual accusations about those who had won prizes in the show tents. This one, it was stated, had bought his winning gooseberries in Gloucester market, the lady who had won the sweet pea competition had never grown a flower in her life, the same people won year after year, the man with the small garden had no chance. And so on. And so on.

The bee-keeping display was the sensation of the afternoon. Unfortunately for him, the expert's bees had not arrived so he had had to borrow a hive of what turned out to be the fiercest black bees that had ever buzzed in the Forest of Dean. They attacked him as if he were their worst enemy, and, in the end, drove him from the gauze tent defeated and in great agony. The poor man's face would have won a prize in the vegetable-marrow class. And yet his humiliation only seemed to amuse the bystanders and convince them more than ever that bee-keeping was a dangerous hobby.

As the sun began to set, and the flowers to wilt, so dancing began at the lower end of the field. The children were now being lugged off home and the crowds began to thin. Last of all there was the ox roasting with slices of juicy beef at 6d. a time, and gluttony triumphant. I was so exhausted I could hardly stand, though I still had to see that the marquees were emptied before being taken down. Emery, as cool as ever, was in the Refreshment tent with some of his cronies enjoying a late drink. There was the smell of a country flower show in the summer air, the smell of ripeness mingled with hot grass and bread and butter. It had been a long, full day, but in the words of Fred Thomas, whose wife had, at last, won a prize for her table decoration, "It has been a fine show. The best we've ever had. But we'll have a bigger and better one next year." Not for me I thought. I wouldn't be dragooned into it next time. My duties finally done, I dragged myself home carrying a dozen white turnips, two cauliflowers and a bunch of tattered carnations for my mother. On the way I ran into "Silly" Ted, our local idiot. He grinned at me and wagged his grotesque head. I patted him good-humouredly on the back and then pinned my Assistant Secretary's badge in his cap.

When I got home, my grandfather was still in the kitchen, banging his cider mug on the table, and grumbling to my mother about the judges. "What a way to run a Flower Show," he muttered, as I staggered off to bed.

9 THE GENERALISSIMO

It happened when I was in my early 'teens, during the Great War of 1914-1918. I was a Boy Scout at the time, the smallest, but certainly the keenest, member of our school troop. Our town had organised yet another flag day in aid of the Red Cross. We scouts were, of course, conscripted. Friends and neighbours were once more to be cajoled and threatened. But I could not bear the thought of begging yet again from the people I knew. I could see their faces falling when I asked them, for the tenth time, to support "our brave, wounded heroes". I almost became a deserter from the troop but the thought that I might soon be promoted to patrol leader was enough to stop me from taking this rash step. Then I had a brilliant idea. I would not go forth into the town with my little shiny, paper flags and converted cocoa tin. I would spare my family and friends. Instead, I decided to make a base of the little railway station at Newnham-on-Severn. Trains stopped there on their way to and from South Wales to Gloucester and London. They waited just long enough, I knew, for me to raid the first-class carriages for contributions. I took the precaution, though, of saying nothing about my plan to anyone except my mother.

So, dressed in my uniform (the shorts were always a little too long for me and the hat too big) I collected my tin and tray of flags from my scout master and made off over the fields and down into the valley where the little wayside station lay. I got there just before midday. My dinner consisted of a hunk of cheese and some doughcake, some early-ripening hazelnuts pulled from the hedges on the way down, and a pound of half-ripe Victoria plums which I had bought from a cottage for threepence. I did well with my flags. The trouble was that none of the trains halted long enough for me to do all the carriages. As I waited for each train to come out of the tunnel I talked to the two porters who told me what trains were expresses and did not stop, and which were not, and did. They were very amused at my enterprise. All the same, I didn't let them off, either, for they sported my little red crosses in their hats before the day was very old.

At about 3 o'clock, and the air sleepy with summer, a long train pulled in from South Wales, bound, as I could plainly read on the board over one of the carriages, for Gloucester, Stroud, Swindon, Reading and Paddington. Almost as if heaven were on my side, a first-class carriage stopped exactly opposite me. Its window was down, so I rushed forward and pushed my head through the opening. I saw three men sitting in the carriage. They were dressed in blue uniforms, with peaked, flat-topped hats on their heads. I knew at once that they were French officers. Two were sitting on one side of the carriage; the other, an older man, had the whole of his side to himself. The cushions were littered with papers. "Will you buy a flag for the Red Cross, sir?" I pleaded.

The man sitting by himself turned to me, smiled very gently and said, "Come in, boy."

One of the others rose quickly and said rather sharply, "No, no."

But I had beaten him to it. I had opened the door and nipped into the carriage. I placed myself in front of the man who had spoken first, and gave the smartest scout salute I could muster. He acknowledged it with an even smarter one and then took hold of my hand. I liked the look of him. He was short, with sharp but kindly eyes, a palish face with rather high cheekbones and a bristling, waxed moustache. I have never been so close to an officer before.

"You are a scout, eh? Have you collected a lot of money?" He had a marked foreign accent.

"Not enough, sir," I replied.

He chuckled. "Well, be quick. Give me a flag."

Without further ado I stuck one in his lapel. He took out a pound note from a wallet in his tunic and pushed it firmly into my tin. I gasped, and saluted again. He smiled again. Then the meeting was cut short, for I heard the guard's whistle and beat a hasty retreat from the carriage. As the train steamed out, the old man bowed his head and lightly waved to me. I stood solemnly to attention—alone but for one of the porters and the stationmaster—on that platform and saluted him for the last time. Hollyhocks at my back were in full flower; white clouds rolled high over in the English sky. My heart beat wild with joy. I had sold a flag for a pound; I had spoken to an officer; I had, in fact, seen three officers; French, too. As soon as the train was out of sight I made uphill for home.

Naturally, I wanted to tell mother first of all about my adventure, but when, at last, I arrived on our doorstep, hot, flushed and over-excited, she was not in. Instead, there was a note left for me, scrawled on a piece of cardboard, and propped against one of the brass candlesticks on the mantelpiece. "Gone to missionary meeting. Cat fed. Where have you been?" Well, I thought, I was not going to put my nose into the middle of that lot gassing in the parish room, so, I went off to our scout headquarters—the front parlour of our scoutmaster's house. When I got there, there were three or four other scouts having their tins emptied. I hardly gave them a chance to receive their proper congratulations. I couldn't contain myself, but burst in with, "I've got quids and quids in mine. A French officer gave me a Bradbury on Newnham Station."

Unbelieving ears listened; doubting eyes looked me up and down.

"Liar," whispered the leader of the wolf patrol, under his breath. But I had my triumph, nevertheless, when my money was counted—£1 7s. 2d., a new pound note, the rest in silver and copper. Then I told them the whole story.

That could have been the end of it. But the next morning, while I was glancing through the newspaper, mainly to see if there were any first-class cricket going on anywhere, I spotted a photograph of a soldier. And it was a picture of the French officer who had put the pound note into my tin. Underneath it were the words "Field-Marshal Foch, who arrived in London yesterday evening for military discussions." There was no mistaking the face. Foch. So I had been saluted by the Commander-in-Chief of the Allied Armies in the Field. I have never felt so proud. The more I thought about it the more I was convinced that the officer was Foch. And years afterwards I proved it was. I discovered, while reading a book about the war, that on one occasion he did come to London, via Cardiff, in order to deceive the German Intelligence Service, who were expecting him to make the normal Channel crossing. And by that curious crossing of paths which happens when least expected, a small boy scout had spoken with a great soldier on an almost unknown country railway station. Good kind man that he was, Foch had not snubbed the boy nor refused to support the cause for which he was pleading.

There is a postscript to all this. I had hoped that having done so well for the Red Cross, and being treated almost as an equal by a Field-Marshal, I should be immediately promoted to patrol leader. But, alas, the ways of scoutmasters are strange. I had to wait a whole year for this. And at the time I couldn't understand why. I thought it vastly unfair.

10 MEXICO

I ONCE knew an old man called "Mexico". He was not more than five and a half feet tall, just tall enough, so everybody said, for him to be able to crane his neck over the vicarage wall to see how the asparagus was getting on. He was broad and thick-set with it, too, so that he did not find it easy to force himself through the belly-squasher stiles of our district. This oak-like west-countryman was christened William, though everybody called him "Mexico"; when I first knew him he was drawing his old-age pension. I have a memory of a pair of eyes, blue as forget-me-nots in April, smiling at me, of an earth-brown wagging finger, and of a smell of burning which, as I later learned, always surrounded him after he had had his whiskers singed. He rarely wore a hat, though on rainy days he pulled on a shapeless tweed cap which he had bought for ninepence from a packman before the turn of the century. On the hottest days he covered his scalp with a large red-and-white spotted handkerchief, knotted at the four corners. Then he might have been mistaken for a pirate or gypsy, and would not have felt insulted. On very special occasions he resurrected his best hat and crowned himself with a smart bowler which he had worn for the first time on his wedding day. His suits were always of the heaviest serge, and the trousers uncreased, for he disdained anything "fancy". Most times he clumped about in hob-nailed boots, fortified at toe and heel with steel protectors, though he kept a pair of best shoes wrapped up in newspaper under the bed to go with the bowler hat. He swore by Welsh flannel shirts, and considered collars to be sops to convention. He was, in fact, in and out of fashion at the same time.

"Mexico's" lobster-red face was strong and determined. His wife claimed that she married him because she knew his chin would never let them down, but in his hearing she used to tell him that it was because he looked so helpless. But I have rarely seen any face with a more mischievous grin. Impishness danced out of his eyes, and seemed to settle in every crevice of his puckered skin. The lips were kind, the ears large and mottled, and the hands rather tiny for a man of his build. Yet, in their time, they had done some pretty heavy work. When fired by summer cider into proud talking, he used to scratch his blistering Roman nose and inform us, with suitable gestures, that when he was younger he could punch a hole through a hundredweight sack of flour. Yet no hands cradled new birds' eggs or bruised butterflies more gently.

"Mexico's" speech was bright and racy, full of electric words of his own invention. His voice was generally low and quiet, and he spoke with the lilting burr of our countryside. He was suspicious of what he called "the talk of the 'igh-ups". It was his custom to refer to the unfortunate inmates of a nearby Inebriates' Home as "the nebites", and he always called a certain brand of boot polish, "unnykew", when other people called it "unique". Of cant and insincerity, he said, "I can't abide hypercrosity, nor ingratitude." His sensibilities were delicate, but once roused he spared no one's feelings. He felled with a word,

We took to each other from the beginning. He adopted me, and I was fascinated by him, for I never knew what he was going to be up to next. If, by some error of time, we had not missed a couple of generations, we should have grown up together, inseparable friends. But time relented and, until he died, we spent many hours in each other's company. When I only reached up to his knees I used to love watching him murdering the long grass in the orchard with a scythe, or mending broken ladders and wheelbarrows, for he was very handy with his hands and had an inventor's mind as well as a poet's speech. He was the fastest plum-picker for miles around. He could swim, tickle trout, make whistles, and play the mouth-organ. It was "Mexico", bless him, who introduced me to the delights of early morning mushrooming and to autumn blackberrying. He placed me on familiar terms with pigs in sties, and horses in fields. The countryside was his world. He came to London once on a day's excursion, but said afterwards that he didn't think much of the place because the beer was too flat and the women too thin. He had two passions which never deserted him, gardening and cricket. There was a third passion, his wife, but you would not have thought so if you had heard him talk about her in her presence but, though he would stoutly deny it, he was her complete slave.

He gardened until he was over eighty years of age. The weather never deterred him, but he waged ceaseless warfare on cats, slugs and starlings. "Get off that bloody garden," he used to bellow when he saw our cat, Sunbeam, sitting smugly in the middle of a row of new peas. "If I can get my hands on you, madam, I'll wring your bleeding neck." And this from a man who hesitated to kill a fly. And about slugs, "He slipped up a bit when He made *them*." And about starlings, "I'd sing hallelujah if I had that lot on a griddle iron." He only considered himself to be a vegetable gardener, his specialities being the growing of elephantine runner beans and mammoth parsnips. He refused to have anything to do with tomatoes.

"Like eating a mouthful of dirt," he used to mutter. What memories I have of him digging grave-deep trenches for his celery, putting battered old buckets upside down on the rhubarb to force it in time for a pie on Easter Day, or waiting patiently in the lane outside for the baker's horse to pass and leave behind some precious horticultural offering. The growing of flowers he left to Mrs. "Mexico", though he couldn't resist interrupting her when she was at work on the borders. I can see her now in black straw hat and veil, brandishing a pair of shears at him when he had suddenly leaned over her shoulder and said, as she snipped away at the privet hedge, "That's not the way to trim a 'edge, woman." "I'll trim you if you don't get on with your business," she savagely countered. He attended every flower show for miles around, making caustic comments on everybody's produce. One year, the local show committee, wishing to acknowledge his years and experience, appointed him a judge. But as he stubbornly refused to award any first prizes, he was never invited to act in that capacity again. He spent most of the time walking round the show tent placing "Third Prize" and "Highly Commended" cards on all the best exhibits. One of the most memorable days in his life, was when he went on an outing to Shrewsbury to see its famous flower show. He got up at three in the morning, walked four and a half miles to the nearest railway station, caught the train to Shrewsbury, spent the whole day at the show, got into conversation with a retired royal gardener, put him in his place, ate four mighty ham sandwiches, left Shrewsbury at sundown, missed his connection at Birmingham, and got back home exactly twenty-five hours later. At breakfast the next morning he presented Mrs. "Mexico" with a bunch of hothouse grapes, a fistful of catalogues and the return half of his railway ticket.

As for cricket, he spent most of the winter talking about it and, until he was well over fifty, all the summer playing it. He gave up, not because he couldn't run, but because he couldn't see the ball. He was of the old school of cricketers. Nyren would have delighted in him. He used the two-eyed stance and pointed his toe at the bowler. He bowled lobs and round-arms, perfect in length, cunning in flight. At one time he was unpaid groundsman to the local club, which meant that he spent most of his time on hands and knees grubbing up daisies and plantains. When a horse was available the pitch got rolled with the large iron roller which had been cast in 1881. When there was not, we boys were pressed into service, seduced, as I well know, by promises of being picked to play in the match the following Saturday afternoon.

When I was about eight years old, he asked if he could take me into Gloucester to see the county team play. Mother knew perfectly well that I should be safe with him, but she had to protest. Her parting shots were, for him, "And don't get taking him into one of them dirty pubs," and, for me, "And no guzzling pop, mind." I cannot remember a single detail of the match. Years later, I discovered that it was against Hampshire, that Dipper made a patient 70 not out, that Phil Mead wore Dennett to a shadow. But I have vivid memories of being taken across the field at tea-time to the pavilion. "Do you see that man there with his head in his hands?" said "Mexico", pointing to a slouched figure who, with long beard and bushy eyebrows, sat with hands clasped over an enormous walking stick. "Well, that's the old man himself. That's W.G., W. G. Grace. And don't you bloody well never forget it." And then, to my surprise and amazement, he fetched me such a wallop that it has served to remind me forever of Dr. W. G. Grace, and of the summer sunshine of that far-off Edwardian day. "Mexico" was never a first-class player—he was too impatient—but none loved the game better, nor all its associations. I think that gardening and cricket are comfortable bedfellows in any part of England. Certainly they were a large part of his Gloucestershire make-up.

As I got older I learned more about him in his early years. He had been born in a cottage in a Cotswold hamlet, the last but one of a cricket team of children. He left school before he was eleven and went bird-scaring at 3d. a day. Then he became a farm labourer and later, hoping to make his fortune, emigrated to Mexico, where, as a platelayer, he helped to build the Mexican State Railways. He was in Mexico for three years, made good money, saved hard, came home and got married. I was brought up on the stories of his adventures, of how he had made friends with the Indians, of roistering expeditions to Vera Cruz, of an Irishwoman who used to make him cups of tea in a land of coffee, of snakes, poisoned arrows, alligator-haunted rivers, and jungles. So gripping were his accounts of fights and gamblings, of silver mining on the sly, and of how the iron road was built from coast to coast, that they have remained with me ever since. I have inherited his lore.

Once having tasted romance, he could never return to the Cotswolds, so he came to live in the Forest of Dean, where he became a blacksmith at one of the collieries. In no time he became foreman of the shop. When the time came for "Mexico" to retire, as if he could ever have retired from anything, he was given a farewell party in the bar parlour of one of the local pubs. When called upon to make a speech, he gave the assembled company three instead. One told them how to grow kidney beans, another gave advice to the selectors on how Gloucestershire could win the cricket championship that year, and the third slated his employers for dispensing with his services at the premature age of seventy. That farewell party has gone down into local history. Apart from the presentation to him of the ugliest marble clock ever made by human hand, the proceedings also included some spectacular drinking, an impromptu concert, and an unsolicited exhibition of cucumber eating. The merry company included a gentleman, who, after consuming more liquor than was good for him, stood up and declared that he could eat a yard of cucumber at one sitting. "Mexico", telling me the story afterwards, said, "Albert always a silly old fool, but not wanting to spoil the pleasantness of the evening, I bet him half a crown he couldn't do it. The landlord produced two and a half cucumbers, we measured 'em up, and sure enough, Albert ate 'em, skin and all. We watched him, hypnotized. He never stopped once. He just went on, chewing and chewing. He swallowed the lot, drank a pint of bitter, said 'ah', and half an hour later fell off his chair. He groaned all the way to Gloucester Infirmary. They operated, and he got better, but he was never the same man after that. Always looked a bit strange. What is more, he done it for nothing, for I forgot to give him his half a crown."

"Mexico" died when the lilac, or the "laylac" as he called it, was first coming into bloom. He knew he was dying, but he hated the thought of leaving everything, and he fussed about some jobs which he had left half finished. He fretted about his garden and asked every day if the new chickens had hatched, and if the apple "blow" had set. The last time I saw him he was propped up in bed, and his breathing was bad. His old face was shrunken to a withered apple. There were dark circles, like black half-moons, under his eyes, and his beard, white as pear blossom, flowed from his face over on to the bedclothes. "Well," and he smiled at me, "and how many did you make last week? How are you getting on at that Monmouth School? Mind you be a good boy and remember what they learn you."

I should think that every man, woman and child, from miles around came to "Mexico's" funeral. The hearse, drawn by four horses, shone in the sun. At least, the black patches of it which were still visible, shone, for wreaths, anchors, crosses, and broken harps were festooned all over it. Behind, there streamed a mile-long procession of mourning. Along the country roads they went. His wife stayed at home and read the Burial Service by herself in her own room. And when they buried him, an English gentleman in Gloucestershire earth, a blackbird began singing in one of the churchyard elms. The Vicar said something about the labourer being worthy of his hire, and of a golden crown. Out of the corner of my eye I caught the blank face of the man who had eaten the yard of cucumber and, rescued from death, was still hoping to receive, no doubt, at that late stage, the half crown my grandfather had promised him.

11 JOSIE

I FELL in love with Josie on Christmas Eve. I had left school the previous July. Josie told me she was eighteen but she turned out to be sixteen. She looked eighteen, though, for she had put her hair up and was wearing high-heeled shoes. I had never even heard of her before. It was Clara Meek who brought her along to the carol-singing. The school choir and some of the old scholars used to go out every year. Josie lived in Cheltenham but was staying with Clara over the Christmas. She had soft, brown eyes, a husky, well-off voice with no trace of our Forest accent, she smelt of scented soap and carried a black silk vanity bag. I thought she was wonderful.

We went carol-singing round the district in aid of our local hospital. We had had a few practices beforehand with Miss Fenley, our French mistress, who conducted us. She had done her best to lick us into some kind of shape though we always remained more of a bawling rabble than a melodious choir.

The girls weren't bad, I'll say that for them, but there were some very doubtful tenors and basses amongst the boys. Les Fox, who was already sprouting a moustache, called himself a bass, but stayed on one miserable note for most of the time. Frankie Burrows, who was better on the football field than anywhere else, began singing each carol as a tenor but generally finished an octave or so lower as a bass. As for Cyril Ireland, I do not know what he was doing with us at all. He did not take any of it seriously. I do not think he piped a note throughout the whole evening, but just pulled funny faces at the rest of us when we were doing our best to please Miss Fenley. It was Vincent Knight, a real musician, and now a Doctor of it, who kept the boys together, and he only did that by insulting us from time to time. Arthur Phelps, who had left school years ago, and was working in the bank, trudged round with us and did the collecting. He was so keen on the old school that he not only sported his old scholar's blazer in December but also used to threaten people with his fist if they did not put what he knew they could afford into the box. The Prince of Peace never had a more militant disciple.

We met that Christmas Eve outside the school. About twenty of us turned up. Over half were girls but I had eyes only for Josie. It had been bitterly cold for a couple of days and all the ponds were frozen over. As soon as we moved off on our rounds it started to snow. Some of us carried stable lanterns so that we could read our music; others had flash-lamps. But the lanterns were always going out and the flash-lamps must have had a number of dud batteries.

We sang *Good Christian Men, Rejoice* outside the police station, and then Arthur Phelps banged the knocker so loudly that we wondered if he was going to break the place down. Inspector Howells answered the door in a bit of a temper, gave Arthur a wicked look, and then put something in the box. Arthur looked at one time as if he was going to raise his fist to him. But we got away without any fuss.

Soon our little company looked like walking snowmen. At first Josie did not take much notice of me, but after we had given the customers of *The Seven Stars*, *We Three Kings of Orient Are*, she asked me my name. By the time we had reached the vicarage I was standing by her side. Vincent Knight said something about not disturbing the balance, but I took no notice of him. We sang *Sleep, Holy Child*, on the vicarage lawn, but the Vicar dashed out, thanked us, put something in Arthur's box and spluttered out something about preferring it if we didn't sing any more carols because of waking the baby up. Apparently Mrs. Vicar was out visiting.

The lanterns went before us when it came to our stumping along the Gloucestershire lanes and over the whitening fields. They flickered like will-o'-the-wisps when they disappeared into the hollows and then came to life again on the tops of the ridges. The hedges dropped snow on us when we brushed against them. Our faces glowed. Josie looked like a frost princess. I felt there was a birth in the air, that this really was the eve of Christmas. No angel sang the praises of the night with fuller heart than I.

We drank hot lemonade at one of our teacher's houses and, as we stood in the porch there, I caught hold of Josie's hand. My glasses were all steamed up, though, so I don't think she saw how happy I was. We finished the carol-singing near the War Memorial with *The Holly and the Ivy* and then broke up for the evening.

I got Wilf Parker to look after Clara Meek while I walked Josie back home. We did not say much but my heart was beating fast. I would have stood on my head in the snow if she had asked me, or taken off my overcoat and put it round her, or something like that.

Before I said goodnight to her, I asked her if she would be coming to church on Christmas Day and if she would meet me after. But as I said it I remembered that Clara was Chapel.

Josie would not promise anything but said she would do her best.

When I got back home mother was waiting up for me in the kitchen. She had stuffed the fowl, made the mince pies, and was now tying the Christmas puddings up in their cloths. The light from the oil lamp fell softly on the supper table, the fire in the grate was still burning brightly, the sitting-room was dark, but I knew it was hung with holly and mistletoe. I stared into the fire and sighed. Mother said, "What's wrong with *you*? You're quiet tonight." I could not tell her what I was feeling. She would not have understood.

She douted the lamp and we went upstairs to bed. Before I fell asleep, Littledean Church bells began to ring Christmas in, over the snow-thick fields. I prayed that Josie would be in church next day. George Trigg's donkey hee-hawed on the skyline.

Josie *was* there; and half the parish with her. We had the same old Christmas hymns and prayers, there was a very short sermon from the Vicar and our organist played us out with a life-like imitation of Christmas bells mixed up with old carols. Somehow or other Josie had persuaded Clara to come with her. They sat together in their finery in the very back pew. When the choir got back to the vestry there was sixpence for each boy and two shillings for each man. I hardly stopped for my Christmas box but pelted off to where the girls were waiting together outside the church. I informed them both, with some pride, that mother had given me a copy of *The Oxford Book of Verse*. I was a bit hurt, though, when Josie grinned and Clara sniffed. Then Clara moved off down the street to leave me alone with Josie for a few minutes. I gave her two small rosebuds from our garden and a new handkerchief which I had forced out of my mother with doubtful explanation. Although Josie did not give me any presents she promised to come for a short walk with me that afternoon. That was bliss enough.

F

As mother and I were washing up after our Christmas dinner, the town's Silver Prize Band struck up in the street outside with *God Rest Ye Merry, Gentlemen*. We were their last calling place. The drummer could hardly stand. The trombone player was all over the place. They had played outside six pubs that morning.

Then I cruelly deserted mother and left her, to sit with her memories, by the log fire. I made for the trysting place.

Josie was half an hour late and said she could not go very far because Clara wouldn't like it. So we just strolled to the edge of the birdless woods. I read her a carol I had written and she told me she was going to help her father in his sweetshop when she left school. She must have found my chatter rather boring for she said she could not meet me the next day. So I went home and read all the love poems I could find in *The Oxford Book of Verse*.

Boxing Day dragged. There was no post and no paper. But that afternoon I played in the annual Christmas hockey match between the School and the Old Scholars. They had cleared some of the snow off the pitch and the ground was not too hard. I had never been much good at hockey at school so the Old Scholars put me in goal. The School beat us easily enough, but I nearly brained the new geography master, got myself plastered with mud and only let three goals through. I also told a few of the opposing forwards exactly what I thought of them. Josie was on the touch line with Clara but, to my dismay, did not take the slightest notice of me. What had I done, then? Why did not somebody tell her that I had never played in goal before? Perhaps she did not like what I called the opposing forwards. I did not see her after the match, and she was not at Dorothy Guest's tea party, either, though she had been invited. Dorothy and her family took a great deal of trouble, but I did not enjoy myself very much, not even when we played Postman's Knock.

Mother had some friends coming in that evening, so I did

not mind leaving her and going with Bob Whitehouse to the
Boxing Day Dance over in St. John's schoolroom. I knew Josie
would be coming, for Wilf Parker had told me he would be
taking Clara. Joe Pope's Band was going to play that evening
—all three of them, Joe at the piano, Sid Smith with his fiddle,
and Alex Griffin on the drums; sometimes Sid Smith played
the sax as well. I started getting ready at 6.30, for Bob was going
to call for me at 7.30. Mother was downstairs cutting ham
sandwiches, with our cat mewing hopefully around her. I put
on my Sunday suit, of course, and my fancy socks. My hair
was plastered down with "Kozo" and I did not forget to take
some Russian cigarettes. Bob had promised to bring some
Turkish fags. So we were well set.

I was just forcing my dancing pumps into my overcoat
pocket when Bob called up the stairs, "Come on, old 'un, get
a move on. We shall be late."

We set off into the night. There was snow in the air again
and a frosty halo round the moon. The front windows of every
house were lit up and we caught a quick sight of rooms decor-
ated with evergreens and grown-ups and children with paper
hats on. When we passed *The White Hart*, there was singing
going on in the bar parlour; Jess Brobyn was giving them a
tearful rendering of *The Mistletoe Bough*. At the bottom of
the hill we caught up with Redvers Jackson, the pump man at
the colliery, just going on the night shift. "Happy Christmas,
Redvers," we greeted him with. "Coming to the dance?"
"What?" he answered, "in these boots? I could give both of
thee a bit of a dance where I be going to now." The sound of his
pit boots echoed on a long time after he had disappeared out of
sight.

But I did not enjoy that Boxing Day Dance though there
were balloons, carnival novelties, competitions, and hot meat
pies in the interval. Josie was there in a pink and white dress
and silver shoes. She hardly looked at me. She danced most of
the evening with Paul Edwards. I only had one slow foxtrot

with her. She was a marvellous dancer. When I told her I had written a poem about her she burst out laughing. I asked her for the last dance but she said she had promised it to someone else. And I couldn't take her home, either, because she was going with Paul Edwards on the back of his motor bike. I was shattered. I could have murdered Paul. To make matters worse, I won the booby prize in one of the competitions and it was Josie who was chosen by the M.C. to give it to me. It was a lemon.

I went home by myself, for Bob had got himself tied up with a girl from Coleford. I never saw Josie again, for she went back to Cheltenham next day. It took me a few weeks to get over her.

I got some satisfaction, though, later on, when Paul Edwards told me that Josie had jilted him. He used to go into Cheltenham on his motor bike to see her. I believe she married a chap from Gloucester in the end and settled down with him in her father's sweetshop.

12 THE CONCERT

THE concert was my idea. And even after all these years I have never been allowed to forget it by my contemporaries. There can never have been a concert like it before. Certainly not in our town. Nor since, either, I should imagine.

I was a member of the Young Men's Bible Class at the time. We were all about fifteen years old; "Young Men" flattered us. We met every Sunday afternoon in the parish room to talk about other things beside the Bible, including the fortunes of the county cricket club, the town football team and the merits of our various girl friends. It was a very successful class with a high percentage of attendance. Charles Tringham, the chief reporter for the local paper, took us and we gave him a high old time of it. But he was a sweet and patient man and seemed to know most things about growing lads.

I thought it would be a good idea to raise money for the annual choir outing. We were all members of the church choir, too. Stanley suggested a jumble sale, but the parish had had three of them already that year. Harry wanted to have a house-to-house collection, but the rest of us had memories of carol-singing at certain houses at Christmas and did not want any more sarcastic remarks and black looks. Fred was all for asking Richard Westaway, the rich grocer, for the lot, but was not willing to do the asking himself. I said that we ought to have a concert so that we could all take part in it. This was thought to be brilliant.

So we formed a small Committee—Stanley, Harry, Fred and me—and met at my house to plan the campaign. First there was the matter of the tickets. Fred thought about 500—100 at 3d. and 400 at 6d.—until we pointed out that the parish room would only seat 300. "Then let the rest of 'em stand," muttered Fred.

"And," said Harry, "can you see 400 willing to pay 6d. to come and look at us?"

So it had to be the other way round. We decided on 200 at 3d. (red tickets) and 100 at 6d. (white tickets). "Of course," I said, "we shall have to have them printed."

"Oh, I'll do 'em," offered Stanley, "on my printing set at home."

"That's no good," said Harry, "you 'aven't got half the letters. And what you 'ave got don't come out plain."

I stopped further argument by saying that I had got a brain-wave.

"What, another?" said Fred. "What is it this time?"

"Let's get old Tringham to do 'em for us cheap at the Mercury office."

Everybody agreed. We fixed on the date of the concert and Charles Tringham said he would do the tickets for us.

Then we went to see the Vicar. Yes, we could have the concert and the parish room, but we should have to tip the verger and leave the place in order. But we could not have the concert on the evening we had decided on because the missionary boxes were going to be opened that night. We could have it on the next night. I suddenly realised the tickets might already be printed. I rushed off to the *Mercury* offices and got there just in time.

Then the committee met again—this time at Harry's house —to decide on the programme. There was a lot of bad feeling about this, but the matter was settled in the end, and when we had got it all down on paper it looked rather imposing. The first half would begin with a solo by Charlie Walding, our blind organist, to give the concert a good send-off. Next, there would be a recitation by Frances Runicles, who knew hundreds of pieces, then a fiddle solo by a friend of the Vicar's who happened to be staying at the vicarage that week, then a funny song by Dan Dorrington, who always brought the house down, then a glee by the men of the choir, a sketch by the girls' Bible Class, and, finally, a magic lantern show by the curate. This would bring us up to the interval. Fred was all for selling sherbet dabs, locust beans, and tiger nuts in the interval, but the rest of us were dead against it. We could not see old Mrs. Partridge trying to cope with a locust bean, or Edgar White, who had charge of the Sunday School, sucking at a sherbet dab. We would do the whole of the second half ourselves. It was Stanley's idea that this should be a nigger minstrel show.

We spent the next week selling tickets to people who did not want them, and got the Vicar to announce the concert at all the Sunday services. Tom Ruck, the verger, promised to put the stage up and get the room ready, and the elder Miss Boud said she would be the accompanist for the minstrel show if we would give her the music. That was a bit of a problem. We had not got any music and had to hum half the tunes over to her. "But don't expect me to vamp," she warned us. We borrowed clothes off people for dressing up and I sent away for some stuff for blacking our faces which I saw advertised in a paper at the barber's. What with one thing and another we only managed to get in a couple of rehearsals, though. But that didn't worry us much. We should be all right on the night.

The night came. It was a lovely, starry night in late winter. The parish room was packed and the tortoise stoves were glowing. We had not got any programmes so nobody knew what they were in for. But the curate was willing to introduce each item as it came. The curtains were drawn at 7.15, only a quarter of an hour late, and our concert had begun.

Charles Walding played *The Harmonious Blacksmith* at a good old lick. Not that Bill Fletcher, our local blacksmith, was very harmonious. There wasn't a crustier man in the place. The recitation—about a rescue at sea—went off well, too, except that old Mrs. Partridge, who had heard the poem many times before knew some of the lines off by heart, kept repeating them out loud just a little behind Frances, until Mrs. Williams next to her nudged her and shouted angrily, "Shut up, woman!" But Frances got an encore and gave us the gem of her repertoire, *The Drunkard's Child*. The violin solo was awful. *Chanson* something or other, it was. "More like a lot of cats howling," said Fanny Bateman. To begin with, the Vicar's friend had forgotten to do anything about an accompanist, and, as he only had one copy of the music, he had to play it by himself. But the poor chap's pince-nez kept falling off. He would play a bit and then had to stop to put his glasses on his nose again. The piece never seemed to be coming to an end. Just when we thought it had finished, off would tumble the glasses again. He got into a frightful state of nerves and did not get an encore. As a matter of fact, Jackie Harris, who was doing the curtains, closed them on him. Dan Dorrington was in fine form. He came on first dressed up as a policeman and sang a song which raised the roof. It was a pity, though, that everybody in the audience had to turn round and stare at P.C. Hiley, our new bobby, who was standing at the back. It made the young man blush all over. Dan didn't wait for anybody to call out "encore". He came on again almost immediately, this time dressed up as a parson. But he had been in such a hurry that he still had his policeman's belt on and the truncheon stuck in it. He was met by such a roar that he started laughing himself and could not stop, either, and had to go off without ever finishing the song. I do not think the Vicar approved. Then the men of the choir sang O, Who Will O'er the Downs so Free? but broke down badly in the second verse and had to start again. Before they had finished, they were all glaring angrily at each other, and all through it, Ivor Jones, the bass, bellowed so loud that he drowned the rest of them. What is more, Jack Bishop, who was conducting, beat so fast that the whole thing became such a gallop that they all ended up panting and out of breath. The girls were not bad in their piece, though there was not much of a plot to it. They just seemed to walk on and off and we could not hear half the words.

That brought us to the magic lantern show. Tom Ruck put the gas lights out and the curate told everybody that he was going to show us some of the missionary slides that had been used the night before. But somehow or other the Band of Hope slides got mixed up with the missionary ones, so that halfway through Life in the Congo we were introduced to a red-faced drunk guzzling down bottles of brandy with the caption "Don't touch it", underneath. But it all ended up nicely and I do not think everybody noticed the difference.

During the interval we got ready for the minstrel show. Jackie Harris placed ten chairs in position on the stage, and arranged some scenery behind that which had been used for the missionary evening the night before. This showed a winding river with crocodiles, and palm trees with monkeys and parrots, but it did very well for us. We wore straw boaters, cricket trousers and blazers. We all looked a bit odd, for none of the stuff fitted very well. For instance, I had our doctor's boater (too small), my own trousers, and the Vicar's college blazer (too large). Stanley's hat came well over his eyes, Harry's trousers, though hitched as high as possible, were far too long for him, and Fred's blazer which announced quite falsely that he was a member of the Gasworks' Bowling Club, and must have belonged to a dwarf, eventually split down the back. Little Willie Greenway looked best, until we noticed that the front buttons on his trousers would not remain done up until one of us put it right for him with a needle and cotton. We all blacked our faces and hands with the stuff I had got. It said on the bottle that we had to paint it on and then it would dry in a matter of seconds. Albert Newton was so keen that he painted the whole of his neck and halfway down his chest, as well as his face and hands. I believe he would have done the whole of his body if we had not stopped him. We left white circles round our eyes, and daubed red greasepaint on our lips. And we all carried Charlie Chaplin canes.

When the ten of us got on the stage we were greeted with a mighty clapping of hands. But, alas, the whole show was a complete fiasco. It had not only been badly under-rehearsed, but everything went wrong for us that night. Bits of the scenery fell down, we came in at the wrong time, we threw poor Miss Boud completely off her balance. We accompanied some of the songs with paper and combs but the paper got too wet and we had to throw it away. We forgot some of the jokes and often stood looking blankly at each other. We were all sweating by the time it had finished, because we were so hot in our borrowed clothes. It was pathetic. But the worse we got, the more the audience seemed to enjoy themselves. They all thought it was part of the show. "Well done, boys," smiled the Vicar afterwards. "Very funny." But Miss Boud declared she would never play for us again. But the worst was yet to come.

We could not get the black off. We rubbed, we scrubbed, we used soap, bathbrick, olive oil and turpentine. But none of it made much impression. It had said nothing on the bottle about how to get the black off. The Vicar had to 'phone to the firm in Birmingham who apologised because they had forgotten to send bottles of getting-off stuff in the parcel. But before it arrived we were in a state. There we were, ten black miserable members of the Young Men's Bible Class. We all went home, dodging our mothers wherever possible. But there it all started up again, the rubbing and the scrubbing. Stanley's mother wouldn't speak to mine for a fortnight. "That boy of yours and his bright ideas." Harry's mother got in such a state they had to send for the doctor. Fred's said it served him right for being such a fool. Of course, none of us went out for a couple of days, except by night, and when we did we had our legs pulled by everybody we met. I suppose that all of us got the black off in the end. But I often wonder if Albert Newton, who must now be quite an old gentleman, is still walking round the town, with half a black chest. I sometimes break into a cold sweat when I think of what might have happened if we had let him paint his whole body.

That was the only concert that the Young Men's Bible Class ever gave. The Vicar would not let us have another. But we raised five pounds for the choir outing and then Richard West-away, who had been at the concert, made it up to ten pounds. He said it was worth every penny. And we had a wonderful day at Weston-super-Mare on the proceeds. We even went to see a nigger minstrel show on the sands.

13 THE LION

THE lion belonged to Bostock and Wombwell's menagerie. I
never saw him myself but he was said to be a very fearsome
beast. It all happened a long time before I was born, but I grew
up with the story of the lion's escape on a snowy night in the
autumn in the 1890's. Of course, I knew the menagerie well;
Bostock and Wombwell's was one of my childhood joys. The
famous travelling show of wild beasts often visited my part of
the world in the West Country. Mother used to tell me how it
came into being. Apparently, George Wombwell, a shoemaker
of Soho, with an eye to business, exhibited a couple of boa-
constrictors to an admiring public in 1804. He did so well out
of that simple venture that he forsook his cobbler's last and
took to the road with a menagerie which soon brought him
fame and fortune. George died in 1850—his family kept the
show going, though it split into three travelling menageries—
and I sometimes go and pay homage to him in Highgate

Cemetery where, travelling days over, he lies, a vault of Victorian dust. And as I stand on that bleak hillside beneath mist-hung skies and dripping trees, I see again, with memory's fond eye, the coloured bills which, plastered on all the hoardings of my little town, used to herald the coming of Bostock and Wombwell's menagerie. How I waited in breathless expectancy for the arrival of the strange and exotic beasts from "the steaming forests of darkest Africa, the mysterious rivers of South America, the dense jungles of Asia, and the unconquered seas around the Poles". They were, it seems, to be brought to my very door, almost overnight. I was, in fact, so impressed by what those bills had to say that I used to open our front door cautiously before bedtime and look out into the night to see if any wild animals were roving there. But there was never a one. There was nothing more exciting than Lou, our familiar and peaceful mog. And when the cages rumbled into the town and the menagerie had established itself for the best part of the week on the Railway Meadow, school could not hold me. I hung round until the early doors were opened and, with other mad children, streamed in with loud beating heart to gawk at ape and bear, elephant and tiger. I never hear a lion roar today without thinking of those dark autumn evenings of naphtha-flare and starlight; I catch a whiff again of the mingled smells of animal, ammonia, and sawdust.

But to return to the lion.

There was a dangerous corner not far from our house where the road, winding up from the village of Littledean in the valley, took a sharp right-angled turn before it made the final climb to the top of the hill. Quite apart from the steep gradient and camber it was a desolate spot. Fields and hedges surrounded it, an ancient pack-horse track (said to be haunted) joined it on the other side of the road, there was not a house in sight. It hung almost on the edge of a precipice. Whenever we passed this spot, mother used to say in an awed and hushed voice, "That is where the lion got out," and then she tightened her grip on my hand and hurried me off down the hill.

Bit by bit I got the story out of her. And as I grew up I talked to a few of the old people who told me more. It all sounds so innocent and amusing now, but it was a sensation at the time. It seems that Bostock and Wombwell's wild beast show was billed to arrive during the last week of October. It was making its way from Gloucester into the mining villages of South Wales, and so to winter quarters. Just after it had left the main road to strike into the Forest of Dean, it started to snow, the first flakes of what turned out to be a hard and bitter winter. And it went on snowing. A wind got up and drifts began to pile. The wagons made slow progress up hills that got steeper and steeper. But they pressed grimly on hoping to reach the showground before evening. Still the snow fell and swirled; October had never known such a storm. The showmen walked by the side of the swaying caravans, or held the horses' heads for, by now, the road had become a sheet of glass. Several times they had to halt and take stock of the situation. It was not until just after 6 o'clock that the procession reached Littledean. It was dark now and there were still three or four more miles to go, and all uphill. Those who had made the journey before knew that the worst was yet to come. But with torches burning, the caged animals restless and angry from their jolting ride, the foam-flecked horses straining at the painted wagons, they started on the last lap. Then at the lonely spot I have described it suddenly happened. A horse slipped to its knees, took another with it, a wagon lost balance, slithered into the bank, and then crashed over on to its side. And this wagon was the cage of, what the bills described as, "The fiercest lion in captivity".

The accident threw everybody into confusion. There was pandemonium. Sweating men shouted and rushed here and there in desperation. The animals bellowed and snarled. The homely English air quivered with the unearthly cries of Africa, Asia and America. Flame flickered on falling and fallen snow;

people in houses, half a mile away, about to sit down to an early supper, wondered what all the commotion was about. But Conqueror, "The fiercest lion in captivity", had leapt out through the shattered bars of his cage and was away into the night with half the menagerie's hands in pursuit. Some remember seeing them running across the snowy fields with torches held high, others how the wagons eventually limped into the town to report the escape of a lion at the police station. But though the inspector, sergeant, and both constables turned out immediately with a dozen other of the natives to scour the countryside with shotgun, pitchfork and walking stick, until midnight, Conqueror remained at large.

Morning broke fair and white. By a superhuman feat of nocturnal engineering the menagerie had pulled itself together, and the cages, not yet all unbarred, were ranged in a long oval the whole length of the snow-covered Railway Meadow. The show was going to open as usual to the public at 3 o'clock that afternoon. But one cage was missing. And Conqueror was the great attraction.

The first news of the lion came from our milkman, William Godbeer. Mother told me he took her aside at 7.30 a.m. to say, "You've heard about the lion 'aven't you? Well, I've seen his tracks. Saw 'em in Long's Meadow when I was coming to work this morning." Shortly after breakfast mother's neighbour, Mrs. Whittle, rushed in to say that Mrs. Cox had just heard from Mrs. James that six lions had got out of Bostock and Wombwell's and had already eaten a whole sheep on Popes Hill. Later it turned out that it was not a sheep but a baby; Williams the coalman had seen the bloodstained shawl. But happily this was contradicted before noon. "People shouldn't say such things," said Mrs. Whittle. A dozen rumours flew round the town that morning. According to well-authenticated reports, the lion had been seen at Newnham, Drybrook, Ruardean and Coleford, places miles apart from each other. If some people were to be believed, Conqueror had been seen in all four places at once. A miner returning home from work at Lightmoor Colliery declared that he had seen the beast chasing chickens. A woman at Collafield watched him disappearing into the forest. Matters reached some kind of climax when Sam Jenkins, the town crier, paraded the streets to announce that Bostock and Wombwell's, now appearing on the Railway Meadow, offer a reward of five pounds to anyone giving information leading to the capture of a lion which had escaped the night before and which answered to the name of Conqueror. ("If you can get near him," muttered Sam under his breath.) There was quite a scene that afternoon at the weekly meeting of the Women's Bible Class in the old schoolroom. Miss Rolls, a mild and gentle lady of the lean and angular type, was charitable enough to suggest that the poor beast might starve to death in such weather, and might it not be a Christian act to leave out some food for him? Whereupon Mrs. Lewis crushed her with the remark, "I never heard such a thing. And why not put yourself out? Not that he'd get much off *your* bones."

The menagerie had full houses at both showings. So much so, that the elder Miss Boud at the sweet shop, puffed up and declared that it was all a bit of advertisement and that no lion had ever escaped at all. "You'd put a different face on it, Rachel, if that animal turned up here in the shop," said her younger sister, Minnie.

So ended the first day of Conqueror's freedom. That night the children were sent to bed early. Not that any of them could sleep. But the local pubs were overflowing and everyone had its own bit of local gossip about the lion. A tramp had been attacked in the woods near Bilson. A pair of lovers were prepared to swear on oath that they had felt the lion's hot breath on their necks when they were quietly sitting on the hay in Marsh's loft. George Johnson, ex-private of the Gloucester's, who had spent two days in West Africa *en route* to the Cape of Good Hope in a troopship, became quite an authority on lions, because he boasted that he had seen them in the jungle and knew all their habits. And how to catch them. "The liar," said Frank Bishop, ex-private of the Hereford's.

It was on the second day that "Silly" Ted, who was a bit soft in the head and wasn't allowed to wander very far from his home, strolled into the police station to say, "About that lion what got out. I've seen 'im. I was just a-going to do a herrand when there he was a-walking down our path. I said to 'im, 'What be you a-doing 'ere?' He looked at me and said, 'Hello, Teddy. I got out. I can go where I like.' I said to him, 'You go back home, Bostock.' And he never said another word but just went off down the lane." The sergeant, though, was not prepared to accept Ted's evidence. He snorted and told poor old Ted to clear off. And in any case, what mattered most was not who had seen Conqueror, or where, but how soon Conqueror was going to be captured.

Then word got out that the military were to be sent for from Gloucester. Before evening, so it was said, the soldiers were on their way, marching through the snow in close order, drums beating, standards flying. Then, later, that they were bringing a field gun with them. By nightfall, Evan Evans who worked for the Council, had heard that they couldn't get the gun up Littledean Hill because of the state of the roads, but they were marching on without it. Needless to say no soldier ever turned up that night or any other. But Harry Smedley, the builder, who could always be found in *The White Hart* at any hour of the day or night, turned over a new leaf and became a reformed character. Apparently he had been working out of the district for a few days, and had not heard about Conqueror's escape. On the way home he dropped into the pub for a drink. There was hardly anybody there at the time and everything was nice and quiet. Charlie Dent and Lee Griffiths were sitting on each side of the fire. Alec Cowmeadow, the landlord, was polishing glasses. After a while, Harry slipped out to go round the back. When he came in again his face was far whiter than the snow and he was trembling all over like a jelly. He slumped down on

G

one of the chairs and pushed away his half-drunk mug of cider. Then he startled the company by gasping out, "I be never a-going to touch another drop of that stuff. I finished with it." "What's wrong with it, 'Arry?" said Alec. Harry lifted his arm up and then let it drop limply. "I just seen a lion out there, a girt big lion, with slobbering chops and shining eyes." Charlie and Les stood up. "Eh," they both said together. "Harry's been and seen Conqueror." They rushed out to the back, too, but the lion had gone. But nobody could ever convince Harry that the lion he had seen was a real one. And he was never seen in a pub again.

The menagerie was still doing well. The lion was still news. "Poor thing," wailed Miss Rolls, "He'll have died from exposure." "They've got him all right, but they won't let on," said the elder Miss Boud. And then, quite quietly, on the afternoon of the third day, Conqueror was captured. "Captured" is hardly the word. "Discovered" is nearer the mark. He was discovered by his keeper in the Vicar of Littledean's parlour, lying down and enjoying himself before the fire. The Vicar, who had once been a missionary in Persia, said that the animal had just trotted in that morning. "He wasn't a bit fierce. He didn't growl at me. So I gave him my dinner, a leg of pork, and then sent a message to the police station. When he'd finished eating the leg of pork, I gave him another, for I'd just killed a pig. Then he just lay down where you see him now. And I've been reading the Bible to him." And the Vicar's name was the Reverend Lamb. And when they came to take Conqueror away, they had no bother to get him to his new cage. The Vicar tickled his ear, as a matter of fact. Then the joke of it suddenly struck all of them. For they had seen the lion lying down with the lamb.

Nobody will ever know where Conqueror had been for two and a half days, or how he had kept himself alive. The elder Miss Boud said that he had been in the vicarage all the time. And when the menagerie moved on, the town settled down

once more to its country ways. But Conqueror was never forgotten. When Bostock and Wombwell's came a few years
later they had got a new lion, "The fiercest lion in captivity."
And Littledean had a new Vicar. For Mr. Lamb was walking
in heavenly pastures with, is it too much to hope, the lion?

14 AND THE GLORY

I HEARD my first complete performance of Handel's *Messiah* in Gloucester Cathedral nearly forty years ago. I was just twenty, a fledgling teacher. It was given by the Three Choirs of Gloucester, Worcester and Hereford on the last day, as usual, of their ancient Festival. What is more I walked the best part of the fourteen hot September miles from my home in the Forest to the Cathedral in order to hear it.

I knew some of the numbers in the oratorio almost by heart. Charles Walding used to play some of them as voluntaries, Jim Jones, our choirmaster, who had about the best tenor voice in the district, had made me familiar with *Comfort ye* and *Every valley shall be exalted*, and the Baptist Chapel choir, with *And the glory*, *Hallelujah*, and *Worthy is the Lamb*. On a calm spring evening when the wind was in the right direction you could hear the loud bursts of singing rolling high over our town, like clouds of praise, as sixty fervent Baptist voices saluted heaven in their packed conventicle. But I wanted to hear the whole of Messiah with famous soloists, and where better than at the Three Choirs' Festival?

My chance to do so came unexpectedly. Some of my early poems had been printed in the local paper. One of these caught the sympathetic eye of a lady who was on holiday with her sister in a cottage on the edge of the Forest. She wrote to me and invited me to go and see them. I went, half amused, half curious. The ladies turned out to be a strange, entertaining couple, with a passion for music, books, flowers, and bee-keeping. I spent a shouting afternoon with them on a lazy day in my August holidays, for one of the ladies was stone deaf and the other nearly so. They were the unmarried daughters of a long-dead bank manager, who had been something of a public figure at Newnham-on-Severn in the 1880's.

After a mountain of a tea, which included honey and wild strawberry jam, I left them to their silences, but not before they had given me a ticket for Messiah at the Three Choirs' Festival, which was to take place a fortnight hence. I had already seen the bills which advertised the Festival and these informed me that Messiah was going to be sung by the Festival Choir with Flora Woodman, Astra Desmond, John Coates and Robert Radford as soloists, and Dr. Herbert Brewer as conductor.

I trudged back home through tall fern and dying foxgloves and thought about those two old deaf ladies, who wanted me to hear and enjoy Handel's music, whose memories of when they last heard it must have been at Festivals long before I was born. It seemed to me that this was their delicate thanks for my poor little poem. So, before I struck the high road again, it was as if the glory of the Lord had been revealed in that woodland, that the mouth of the Lord had spoken it.

It was only when I reached home that I realised, with a pang, that the holidays would soon be over and that I should be back at school on the very Friday of the performance. And I had just been given a passport to paradise. It really was too much to bear.

There was nothing for it, though. I was determined to go to Gloucester at all costs. So I went down to see John Emery to ask him to give me leave of absence. It was as if I was about to enter a lion's den. He listened to what I said, sniffed when I mentioned the two old ladies, glowered at me over the top of his glasses, and then said, "I can't give you permission. You will have to ask the managers. And who is going to take Standard 5 if you go gallivanting off to Gloucester?" More than a little downcast, I went off to see the Chairman of the managers. He was on holiday. His daughter-in-law referred me to the Vice-Chairman. So I strolled over to the other end of the town to have a word with him. His wife told me that he had not yet come home from work. Would I call round later? Undaunted, I called on the Correspondent to the Managers, one of the town's solicitors. I got a fishy-eyed welcome from him, and was advised to send in a letter stating particulars of my "case". Of course, he took good care to point out, I should lose a day's pay, even if I was given permission. But he didn't think I should be allowed to go so early on in the term. And what were the summer holidays for, anyway? And the managers wouldn't be meeting until the second Wednesday in September. So there I was in a frightful dilemma. But I had made up my mind, though I had momentary visions of instant dismissal and everlasting disgrace. When I confided in my mother, her only comment was, "Well, I know you'll please yourself. You always were headstrong." And then with a smile, "I wonder how many other lads there are in Gloucestershire who are thinking of walking all that way just to hear a piece of music?"

The larks had already been singing the glory of the Lord for an hour when I rose at five on the morning of my journey. Mother had borrowed a well-thumbed copy of the vocal score for me from Rachel Boud, who had once been my music teacher, and with this, and a good egg and bacon breakfast inside me, I started out, bold and resolute enough, in the frail sunlight, on my long walk. The hedges were hung with spiders' webs, the grasses heavy with dew in the long meadows, the road was clear before me, the sky wide and empty. There were few people abroad at that hour—a couple of weary miners returning home from the night shift, who nodded and passed the time of day with me, a milkman, just beginning his rounds, a paper-boy whistling from door to door. I caught the sound of a distant shunting train in the valley. Every valley shall be exalted, I said to myself. I passed by farms where cows were already plodding back into the pastures. All else was singing birds with the sun rising higher in the heavens like a slow crescendo. But I did not want for company. I carried Flora Woodman, Astra Desmond, John Coates and Robert Radford with me in my heart and pocket. And it was not Dr. Herbert Brewer, the Cathedral organist, who was conducting the massed choir and orchestra as I walked briskly on. It was me, and I was getting a superb performance, too. I remember how golden the corn-fields were between Littledean and Westbury, "orient and immortal", with the barley ripe for cutting, and the vivid lines of poppies wandering through the bending stalks. At Elton Corner I overtook a dark-eyed tramp on his way to West-bury Workhouse and talked with him until his journey's end. He had slept in Chepstow the night before. Yes, he was very fond of music, and used to sing in a choir in South Wales when he was a young man. But his parents had died, he'd gone to sea, he'd never married, and life had just drifted on like that.

The orchards were heavy and purple with a harvest of glistening plums all the way from Westbury to Chaxhill with spotted pigs chuntering and scampering beneath the loaded trees. The glory of the Lord was suddenly revealed again on the side of a hill with the appearance of a field of mushrooms, like a field of manna. I struck the silver-glinting Severn a mile or so out of Minsterworth. Just before 10 o'clock I picked out the Cathedral tower, through a gap in the hedge, white and shining, six or seven miles away at the foot of the Cotswolds. There I was bound in hope, there I knew they would now be getting ready for the praising day. The best part of the journey was behind me, so I squatted on a heap of stones and had a second breakfast of hazel nuts, blackberries, fallen apples, and the bread and cheese mother had packed for me.

I had a friend, Will Harvey, the poet, who lived in a red brick Georgian house in Minsterworth. I knew that he had written some poems for a song cycle called A Sprig of Shamrock, which Dr. Brewer had set to music for that year's Festival. As I had plenty of time in hand, and Gloucester was in striking distance, I decided to call and see if he was at home. He was not only at home but he welcomed me as if I had been the Prodigal. "Come in, boy. Come in. And where might you be going at this time of day on a new September morning?" When I told him, he broke into peals of laughter, and called out to his mother who was somewhere about the house, "Mother. Where are you? Come and see a prize exhibit. Here's a chap who is walking to music all the way from the Forest." Mrs. Harvey wanted me to have another breakfast but I told her I hadn't time. But Will broke in with, "O, but my sister and I are going into Gloucester by car. We'll give you a lift. Plenty of time. I suppose you've got a ticket."

So there I was sitting down in the Harvey's front parlour, at half past ten on a Friday morning, with dusty shoes and a hole in my right sock, eating a bacon sandwich. And I was only an hour away from Dr. Herbert Brewer, Flora Woodman, Astra Desmond, John Coates, Robert Radford, and the London Symphony Orchestra. It did cross my mind that Standard 5 would now be doing arithmetic. Then Will asked me if I would like to spend the night with them. They were going to have some friends in, there would be music, songs by Ivor Gurney, and probably Herbert Howells playing Bach on the sitting-room piano. Mrs. Harvey promised to get a message to my mother, so I decided to stay the night.

The car dropped us in Westgate Street a few minutes before all the clocks in Gloucester began to warn the city that it was 11 o'clock. There were flags and bunting flying everywhere and great excitement in the festival air. I was tingling with expectancy. College Green, neat and inviting, with its old trees and older houses still drugged by the sleep of centuries, was all top hats and morning dress, as if a royal wedding was about to take place there and then. Cars and carriages came and went, depositing their silken loads. Everyone was happy on that wonderful morning as if kings had come to the brightness of His rising. The little knots and bunches of people were already breaking up and moving steadily into the Cathedral through the south porch and the other doors. I was impatient to get to my place. The Harveys were about to leave me for their seats beneath the great west window when Will suddenly clutched my arm. "Look, boy. Over there by the deanery door. That's Elgar and Bernard Shaw." Spellbound, I watched them as they disappeared into the Cathedral, the tall, saturnine, hatless, knickerbockered playwrite, and the immaculate, stately, trilby-hatted, grey-moustached composer. Just to see them had been worth my long walk, and losing a day's pay—about 6s. Yet, my conscience began to prick me when I thought again of my deserted Standard 5. I wondered what was being said in the staff room about the truant teacher.

I made for my seat in the north aisle. It was now nearly 11.30. I could just see, between the mighty Norman pillars, the massed choir and the London Symphony Orchestra, with the principal first violin, W. H. Reed, waiting patiently for the conductor to appear. The Cathedral was packed, with a subdued rustle of conversation still going on. I looked round in gratitude. I smelt that peculiar must of the ages which old cathedrals have. Shafts of broken sunlight streamed through the windows like prayers flashing from heaven. One patch of red mingled with purple falling on a memorial tablet nearby fascinated me for the whole of the service. The history of my county was written around me on wall and marble tomb. The dead city fathers slept on in their carved urns in sure and certain hope that in their flesh they would see God. The stone cherubs stared at me, eyeless, as if I were no part of their eternity. The man who was sitting next to me seemed to be a white-haired angel.

At last the four soloists came in, and then Dr. Brewer. I could just see a crimson left arm and side, for he was wearing his doctor's robes. The congregation fell to quiet and my heart to a deep thankfulness, as if some blessing were about to fall on me. I was twenty, and the bloom was still on me.

The choir sang an unaccompanied motet, *Hosanna to the Son of David* by Orlando Gibbons. And then, after a short pause, the orchestra struck that noble tonic chord of E minor and, at last, I was listening to *Messiah* in my Cathedral.

I sat enraptured until the end of the morning's performance, for the oratorio was to be sung in two parts. I have no clear recollection of what I did at lunchtime but I know that I was sitting in my place again in the north aisle when the performance began at a quarter to three. My head was full of Handel and history. I remember Astra Desmond telling good tidings to Zion, Robert Radford reminding us of the light that shone on the people that walked in darkness, Flora Woodman lifting us to the vaulted roof as she preached the gospel of peace, and John Coates dashing them in pieces like a potter's vessel. And there were the tremendous waterfalls of harmony from the choir. Hallelujah. Hallelujah. The Kingdom of this world is become the Kingdom of our Lord. When the trumpet sounded, and let loose a flight of echoes, I was raised with the dead, and for that small moment in time, I was changed.

With the final Amens still rolling round the nave, and all through me, we went out into the afternoon sunlight of College Green. I met Will Harvey again who, face transported, was mopping his brow with a red-and-white spotted handkerchief. He stood bare-headed there beneath the soaring tower. He pointed out some of the notables who were talking to their friends—Vaughan Williams, Walford Davies, Granville Bantock, who were all having works performed at that year's Festival. Then some of Harvey's friends joined him. I was introduced to Herbert Howells who had had two new works performed that week and later to Dr. Brewer himself, as the chap who had walked from the Forest that morning to hear *Messiah*. "But," chuckled Harvey, "he hasn't thought of how he is going to get back."

Get back. How to get back—to Standard 5, my Head Master, the Managers, to a day's pay lost. But all that could wait. It was here and now that mattered. I had heard *Messiah* in Gloucester Cathedral in the company of Will Harvey, Bernard Shaw, Sir Edward Elgar, and all the other great ones. And the glory of the Lord was around me.

15 WILL HARVEY

I FIRST met Will Harvey in my last year at school. I was barely seventeen; he was twice my age. I had begun to write—and to have printed in the local paper—what John Emery called "your little bits of verses". One day someone told me that the author of *Ducks*, a poem I knew by heart, lived only a few miles away. I could hardly believe it. I had pictured the writer of that poem living in some remote poet's arcadia. I wrote to him, told him I wrote poetry, and asked if I could come and see him. By return came a creased postcard with a sepia picture of the Severn Bore on one side, and on the other, in jagged handwriting, the magic words "Come next Saturday. Have just seen Parker take eight for forty." Parker was one of my cricketing heroes, the Gloucestershire left-arm spin bowler, then at the height of his magnificent destructive powers. Saturday came. With my notebook of original poems tucked safely into my pocket I cycled, in a dream, all the way downhill to the charmed village of Minsterworth. I kept on reminding myself that I was going to see a real poet. I had once seen a real Field-Marshal and a real live Lord, and had not been disappointed. I got to Minsterworth half an hour too soon, wandered about a bit aimlessly and then knocked at the door of the Georgian house where Will Harvey lived with his newly-married wife, his mother and sister. The great man was not at home. "Would I wait for him in the parlour?" asked his sister. "He's out playing cricket."

"Oh, could I go and see him?" I ventured, rising eagerly from my chair.

"Well, he's at Gloucester."

I sat down again. Gloucester was three or four miles away and I feared that if I left the house I might miss him. Four o'clock came, and no poet. By five we had finished tea. At six, having nothing more to talk about, I thought it was time to go home. Mother would be wondering if I had been drowned in Severn. About a quarter past he arrived, still in his "whites", and breathless with apologies. He had forgotten to tell me about the match. I later learned from a hypnotised eye-witness that he had scattered the spectators with some terrific off-drives, and almost maimed a fielder for life who had been so foolish as to get in the way of a wicked square cut. The truth is that, both as batsman and fielder, Will Harvey was near county class; his bowling, on the other hand, was poetical in the extreme—very slow and not very straight. Before I had left that welcoming household he had glanced at my notebook of poems, said a few kind words about them, toasted our muse in cider, and invited me to come again the following Sunday.

"And there'll be no cricket match this time, I promise you, though we've got our own variety of cricket here—in the house," was what he called after me as I got on my bike to make the long pull uphill back home. They had indeed got a devilish variation of cricket in that house and it had taken a poet to invent it, too. You played Harvey's cricket in a long, narrow court, no more than four feet wide, at the back of the house. There were no wickets but only a high wall behind you. The courtyard also had a roof which covered it for half its length. The ball was a hard one, something in size between a cricket and a fives ball. You hit this, or at least tried to hit it, with a shortened hockey stick. You were out if the ball hit the wall three times. Every visitor to that house who had any interest in cricket was pressed to play that version of the game and whatever the season of the year. It had quite a long list of distinguished casualties, including two cathedral organists (bumps on the head), four county batsmen (broken knuckles) and many of the local farmers (normally black eyes). I begin to ache again when I think of my wild efforts at that savage game.

Will Harvey described himself as "a thickset, dark-haired, dreamy little man, uncouth to see". He had certainly, except on special occasions, a fine disregard for clothes and, when among his own familiars, of razors, also. I remember him best of all ambling along the country roads, wearing a rather stained navy-blue suit, a battered trilby hat planted firmly on his head, gold-rimmed spectacles on nose, and cigarette between tobacco-stained fingers. He was forthright in speech (his expletives were often Chaucerian), he was as tender-hearted as a kitten, humorous, eager, with great powers of endurance, quietly but deeply religious. He was a superb mimic with the kind of expressive face which would have earned him a fortune on the music halls. I can hear his laughter now, and see him, convulsed, taking off his spectacles to wipe the tears of merriment from their lenses with his sleeve. How often did we both hang helplessly on to some roadside tree as we shook and gasped with joy, as between us we went over again the incidents of some anecdote which had caught our fancy. His conversation was as gay as his laughter and as dashing as his cricket.

Until I left Gloucestershire I saw a great deal of Will Harvey. I often used to walk with him to my home from the village of Littledean. This was always on Fridays when the Petty Sessions were held, for Will was a solicitor and in great demand as an advocate. He rarely prosecuted. Everybody in trouble went to him. He would defend widows threatened with eviction from their cottages, girls who, in his racy language, had "slipped a bit", and all those people who, otherwise blameless in their lives, suddenly found themselves on the wrong side of the law. I doubt if the courts of West Gloucestershire ever heard better oratory. I have seen a bench of the most matter-of-fact justices listening entranced as that swarthy, kind little man pleaded passionately that the case against some poor unfortunate should be dismissed.

He talked little about himself, though much about books, cricket and the Cotswold villages—just what I needed at that stage of my life. But one day, sitting comfortably in the snug of a quiet pub by Severnside, he told me something about his life, of how greatly he admired Ivor Gurney, that tragic figure of a fine musician and poet, of how miserable he was when he had to leave his home to serve his articles as a solicitor in Swindon, of how he first began to write poems. As we were chatting, Will began to sing Gurney's rousing setting of Masefield's *Captain Stratton's Fancy*, and of "the old, bold mate of Henry Morgan".

"Of course," he went on, "when the war broke out I enlisted at once, in the 5th Gloucesters, and wrote most of the poems of my first book in the trenches."

I once asked him, very soon after our first meeting, about a huge walking stick he sometimes carried about with him. He chuckled and said that it was a "medal winner". I was mystified until he explained that, in 1915, he had won the D.C.M. for "what they said was conspicuous gallantry". Not long after that conversation I came across the citation as it appeared in *The London Gazette* and which reads, "He and another N.C.O. went out to reconnoitre in the direction of suspected listening posts. In advancing they encountered the hostile post evidently covering a working party in the rear. Corporal Knight at once shot one of the enemy, and, with Lance-Corporal Harvey, rushed the post, shooting two others, and assistance arriving, the enemy fled. Lance-Corporal Harvey pursued, felling one of the retreating Germans with a bludgeon." A funny weapon, I always thought, for such a gentle man, until I began to think

of cricket played with a hockey stick, and his own performances in the field with the bat. I knew, too, that he had been a
prisoner of war for two years in seven different camps; he
must have been a bit of a handful. He wrote some of his best
poems in captivity, and showed me the soiled little exercise
book in which they had been scrawled and which the Germans
allowed him to send home to be published. I never tired of
hearing him tell the story of how he nearly succeeded in escap-
ing by jumping from a train, and of how he and his fellow
prisoners had nearly driven the Germans mad with their antics.
The war over, Will went into practice again and eventually
landed up in the Forest. And there, among the oaks and the
miners, he stayed for the rest of his life.

The Foresters loved every inch of him. They knew he was a
good lawyer, admired his cricket, but most of all enjoyed his
company. A miner once said, "Mr. 'arvey, he's like a lovely,
wicked old gnome. I only has to look at him to bust out laughing." And Will Harvey loved us, and our cottages, and pigs,
and skittle alleys, and male voice choirs. He drank with us in
our pubs, listened to our troubles, told us his, and, though we
did not always know it, gave us free lessons in law and litera-
ture. He made some remarkable broadcasts about us and our
part of England. In fact, he became one of us. He died a poor
man as the world understands riches, but how many he en-
riched with his simple goodness and fidelity.

Will Harvey opened the magic casements of poetry for me.
He bequeathed to me his special joy in Shakespeare, Chaucer
and Hardy. And he fanned my enthusiasm for cricket and
taught me some of its finer points. He was a wonderful
example, too, of a man who learned, through bitter experience,
to be contented with his lot, though life had given him many
disappointments.

The last time I saw Will Harvey was on a serene autumn
day in his village of Yorkley. We walked in the woods during
the golden afternoon, taking with us his two young children,

a sparkling, excited little boy and a shy, elfin girl. The acorns and beech nuts were strewn on the sun-patched turf. A few late foxgloves still flared in the browning bracken. One or two birds sang as if summer was still lingering. At every turn we saw the grey, forest sheep nibbling the grass. The two children ran on, and in and out the undergrowth. Will and I walked and talked and sang. We sang some of the old folk songs and Irish melodies, he with his soft and pleasant baritone and me with my uncertain tenor. The evening mists began to fall, so we went back through the ghostly trees to his home and ate a late tea by the light of a fire glowing with holly logs. He sat at table with his collar off and the light of the table lamp fell on his stubby fingers. Around us were his books, the remnants of what had been once a fine library. The children were put to bed and Will's Irish wife began to tidy up for the night. He got up and fetched a copy of Shakespeare's sonnets from the top of the dresser and began to read one of them out loud. "He's got everything," he said, "and they'll never better him." Then he closed the smooth-covered book, which had been his companion in captivity, and gave it to me. I still have it, with all his comments scribbled over its pages. Then he quietly bowed his head, looked at me over the top of his spectacles, and put his hand on my shoulder with the words, "Well, after all, I did write *Ducks* and they can't take *that* from me." I said goodnight to Mrs. Harvey and then Will and I went out into the darkness. I do not think we said anything else except the usual goodbyes. I got the bus which was to take me back home, and looked through the back window to catch my last sight of him. There he was, smiling at me and waving his old trilby hat. Then he faded into the Forest night. I never saw Will Harvey again. There were a few letters, a few post-cards. I think, perhaps, he never forgave me for leaving Gloucestershire. But Will Harvey, a country character if ever there was one, with a brave, unshackled spirit, wrote the name of poetry on my heart, and for that alone I bless his memory.

H

The literary critics have ignored him, but what a host of ordinary people know and enjoy his poem *Ducks*. Few knew him outside his own county. No poet in this century could have been more local. And yet I believe Gloucestershire folk will honour Will Harvey so long as Gloucester cathedral stands and the river Severn washes the dark slopes of the Forest of Dean.

16 COMING TO LONDON

I was six when I first came up to London. We always spoke of going "up" to London; never "down". But I remember little of that adventure. Certainly nothing at all of the great city itself, but only of my being with mother and of our getting up very early on a summer morning to catch the excursion train to Paddington. I did not associate Paddington with London, though, and wondered why our destination was not called London Station. I have vague memories of seeing a few of my contemporaries with their mothers and fathers waiting impatiently on the platform of our little station for the train to come in, and, later, of a smooth-satined lady who gave me a ham sandwich when we got to Swindon. Although I have forgotten everything else about that incident, I remember the sandwich well enough because I concealed the hated ham fat in my trousers pocket and, alas, forgot to get rid of it. Mother discovered it the day after.

I came to London the second time to see the British Empire Exhibition at Wembley. I travelled up by bus and by myself. I had arranged to meet a girl I had known at school outside the Sarawak pavilion at the Exhibition. Unfortunately, she didn't turn up. She was not very bright at school and it may be that she waited for me outside some other pavilion. As I have not seen her for thirty-five years, she may still be there.

I stayed with some near relations at Streatham for a week but saw little of them because I left for Wembley early every morning and did not get back until late at night. It was in their house that I first heard the wireless. There was a crystal set in my room and I used to lie in bed in the stillness of the night charmed to sleep by the music of Carroll Gibbons and the Savoy Orpheans Band.

I wish I could remember more about the Exhibition. I suppose I must have seen most things there. I know I gave myself the doubtful pleasure of a terrifying ride on the Big Dipper. What has stuck in my memory longest of all is that I met a jovial middle-aged Dutchman called Pieter Vlinck at the Exhibition. Pieter was a variety agent, over in London making arrangements for some of the artists on his books to appear in a new West End revue. With time on his hands he had decided to spend a few hours at the Wembley Exhibition. I ran across him in the Hall of Fame. We got into conversation when he looked at me hopefully and said, "The place to go? You know where?" I didn't understand what he meant at first but gradually the light dawned and I directed him to where he wanted to go. Pieter then invited me to meet him again in Leicester Square for supper that evening after he had carried out a business engagement. "Then," he said, "you will show me London. After, we eat." What he didn't realise was that I had only been in London for a couple of days.

I do not think I shall ever forget that supper. To this day I can see the waitresses staring at us; I can hear them tittering in their corners. For, after we had had our soup, Pieter consulted the menu again, through spectacles with lenses as thick as half-onions, and said to me, "Now I will have the Yorkshire pudding." "What," I murmured, "by itself?" "Ja," went on Pieter, "I have never tasted that pudding." I forgot what I ordered but the pert little waitress gave Pieter a very curious look when she brought him a small portion of Yorkshire pudding. This soon disappeared. "Good," said Pieter, "some more, if you please." A second piece arrived and was as quickly despatched. This embarrassing performance continued until Pieter had got rid of six plates of Yorkshire pudding. I did suggest to him that he might ask for double or treble portions, but he breezily waved me aside and said he preferred to have it in "ones". When he paid the bill it struck me that I had seen a man eat three-and-sixpence-worth of Yorkshire pudding at one sitting. Before I said goodbye to Pieter that night I had whirled him half over London, to have fleeting glances at everything which I could name correctly.

I was twenty-five when I came to London for the third time. I became a teacher in a tough school in Camberwell. I did not find it easy to leave home, but several of my school and college friends were already in London and I looked forward to seeing them in their different setting. Mother had always hoped that I would settle down with her in the countryside of my childhood where, as she said, you know everybody and everybody knows you. She thought of the many temptations of the wicked city, and took it almost for granted that I should be robbed, find my way into bad company and end up in disgrace in the police courts. I had to remind her that I had already been cautioned by our local policeman for tickling trout in forbidden waters. But that did not seem to impress her very much. But, at last, there came the dreadful moment when I grabbed hold of my suitcases, kissed her goodbye and got on the bus which was to take me away from her to London. I had all life before me, and as I watched familiar fields, houses and churches go by, I knew I should see them all again. Not so with mother. She had all her life behind her and I was fairly certain she would go back to the lonely house and sit there in tears.

My first lodgings in London were in a late Victorian house in a quiet road near Peckham Rye. The place had been highly recommended by a friend. When I first saw the green and wooded expanse of Peckham Rye I felt it was rather like being at home.

The lodgings, though, were fantastic. The house was owned by a dowager-looking lady called Mrs. MacMumbo. She was an imposing figure, white-haired and full-bosomed. She was always well dressed even when she was dealing with the pots and pans in her kitchen. When got up for a special occasion she looked very stately and formidable with all her jewellery and finery. But she was a snob through and through. She never ceased to remind us that she considered it rather *infra dig* to take in lodgers. She had, it appeared, fallen on hard times. Her father had been something big in the City, with his own carriage and pair. When he died, he had left her enough money to live comfortably for the rest of her life. She was also well-connected on both her father's and mother's side, and there were still cousins living who were landed gentry. Unfortunately, she had been given some bad advice and had invested her money in a disastrous financial adventure and had lost the lot. "Thousands went in a night," she moaned. So she was forced to take in lodgers. "I used at one time," she told us, "to call them 'paying guests' but I soon found out that a number of them never paid if they could help it. And a few of them I would never have had as guests in father's day. So I prefer to call them 'lodgers'." At no time were any of us ever treated as equals. There were four lodgers in the house in my time. There was Miss Stevens, a lady of uncertain age who spent most of her time "doing things" in her bedroom when she wasn't teaching at a near-by school, a retired parson ("I believe he is a bookie," Mrs. MacMumbo used to whisper to us), who disappeared shortly after breakfast and was not seen for the rest of the day, a gay, black-haired, highly-polished gentleman who worked in one of the local banks, and myself. I was by far the youngest member of the household.

We were always having scenes, especially at breakfast. The parson ate his food gloomily and muttered under his breath whenever Mrs. MacMumbo came near him. The lady teacher sulked and pouted most of the time, and usually did no more than toy with her toast and tea. The chap who worked in the bank, and myself, regularly shared her discarded bacon and egg between us. He had the egg one morning and I the bacon, and so on. Although what we paid Mrs. MacMumbo for our board and lodging was a good average price for those days, she constantly reminded us at breakfast, where she presided as if at a state banquet, that everything cost a great deal, and did we realise how well we were off in her house. We were used to such crushing remarks as, "I thought I had made enough toast, Mr. Gracewell, but apparently not." And, "A good plateful of bacon and eggs is enough for anyone, I think." It was "eggs" in the plural which enraged me.

We were always having crises in that amusing house. I was accused of coming in late night after night (which was perfectly true) and leaving the front door unlocked. "Some people, though educated," complained Mrs. MacMumbo, "are not old enough to be trusted with a front door key." The lady teacher was always complaining that her private letters were being read. Poor old Brightside, the parson, was once accused of burgling his gas meter and was only able to quieten our imperious landlady down by threatening to call in the police. Gracewell so far disgraced himself as to come home slightly drunk one evening. "Disgraceful," said Mrs. MacMumbo when she met him in the hall grinning sheepishly at her, "this is not a public house, Mr. Gracewell. And you the son of a gentleman, and working in a bank." But, for all her irritating ways, Mrs. MacMumbo was a kind-hearted woman who did a lot of good by stealth, though I only discovered that years later.

But I did not spend a great deal of time in those Peckham Rye lodgings, for there was all London to explore. I was not well paid as a teacher, but money went farther in those days and then, as now, there was a lot to see for nothing. I soon got to know Fleet Street and its intriguing alleys, the high dome of St. Paul's, and haunted the bookstalls in the Charing Cross Road. I walked everywhere. I met unemployed poets in Soho pubs, I sent my own poems to *New Verse*, and had them either ignored or returned with a rude note, I went to hear the young David Gascoyne read his poems at the P.E.N. Club, and John Masefield his in St. Martin-in-the-Fields. I went to strange parties in Chelsea where we sat on the floors of muddly flats and talked high-sounding nonsense about art, where scruffy girls sighed as they held the hands of even scruffier boys. I soon had enough of that. I queued at the Old Vic to see the young Gielgud and Peggy Ashcroft, I went to concerts at the old Queen's Hall and cheered Sir Henry Wood until I was hoarse. The Tower, the Zoo, the museums, the National Gallery, the Abbey, the river, the cheap little restaurants—I patronised them all. I was the country boy gone mad. London went to my head.

And then it all palled. I pined for my Forest woods, Severn in bright flood, the great line of the Cotswolds, and my childhood friends. One Friday evening in April I could bear it no longer. I caught the mail train at midnight from Paddington to Gloucester and walked the four miles home, from the little wayside station where I alighted just in time, through the spring night, with the moon glinting on Severn at my back and on the fields I knew and loved on each side of me. I met no one as I plodded up the long hill but I was not lonely. I was home again, and soon I should be sitting down, a returned Prodigal, to breakfast with mother in the familiar kitchen. London was 150 miles away. I knew I should have to return to it on Sunday night. But this was Saturday morning, the larks were soaring, and I felt like a god as I sniffed the budding air.

17 WALTER DE LA MARE

I THINK I must have been about eight or nine when I read a poem called *Silver* in a book which I had bullied my long-suffering mother into buying for me from a stall in Gloucester market. I now know that that book was *Peacock Pie*, first published in 1913. I wrote a letter to the author, "the man with the funny name", addressing it Walter de la Mare, c/o the G.P.O. and objecting to "shoon" (rhyming with "moon") as the plural of "shoes". Most people would not have bothered to answer such a piece of impudence. But not Walter de la Mare. Like the man in Thomas Hardy's poem, he was "a very dear, dark-eyed gentleman" who could never resist a request from a child. In time, he wrote a letter to me in his own defence, justifying the grammar and referring me to Chaucer and Webster's Dictionary, mere names and worlds of mystery to me. But I had fallen under the de la Mare spell. I have been bound apprentice to it ever since.

I did not meet Walter de la Mare in the flesh until he was over seventy years old. "You see in me," he said, "an old-age pensioner, a decaying minstrel." We had been writing to each other for some months and then one day he invited me to take tea with him in his house at Twickenham. I got to know that house very well for I was a welcome visitor to it for over ten years. I explored its bookshelves and enjoyed the treasures of hand and eye which every room held. Each time I went to see Walter de la Mare was a fresh and stimulating experience. Because of his ill-health, I never saw him outside the house, though he was always threatening to come to mine to look at my bookshelves which, at least, contained copies of nearly everything he had ever published in book form.

I cannot pretend to be his Boswell. In my case, I was always too fascinated by him, when in his company, to keep any detailed records of what he said or did. But so many things come back to me now. For all the years I knew him he lived his quiet, ordered life—almost that of a recluse—in an atmosphere deepened and enhanced by all that was gracious and lovely. And that atmosphere contained his devoted "N", who cared for him and nursed him tenderly until the morning of his death. Sometimes I would catch him looking out on his garden, in sight and sound of the Thames, enjoying the blessing of bird-live lawns and butterfly-haunted flower borders. He was especially proud of a huge plane tree, said to be the tallest in England. He missed none of the signs of the changing and returning seasons. A dropped feather, a staring berry, a flake of snow, a clockless snail—and his divining imagination and memory did the rest. He showed me a pane of glass on which Laurence Whistler had engraved that immortal last verse of *Fare Well* which begins "Look thy last on all things lovely". He had signed the words with his familiar signature, holding the appropriate tool with unexpected skill, with the engraver instructing him by his side. Near at hand, for calm fingers to clasp, would often be a pair of binoculars, as if those particular eyes ever needed help to see more clearly. I used to think then of his Miss M. and her telescope. I can remember him sitting in an elegant grandfather chair, or reclining in his bed, surrounded by books and letters, serene and unruffled. When he stood he was seen to be about five feet, eight inches tall, with a head which would have served for the statue of a Roman emperor, so powerful and clear-cut was its modelling. The hair had not yet companioned with the hoar frost. The ears were large and so obviously listening, the lips firm and gentle. As I looked on that face, so wonderfully unlined, and so alive with meaning and purpose, I knew that I should never forget its contours. I did not see it frozen in death, but I was told that it was magnificent, triumphant and happy, and more truly still than anything in life is ever still. But from the first time they weighed me up, it was the dark eyes which attracted. They have often been described as bird-like. But of what bird? The eagle or the robin? They were certainly intense. They missed nothing. They saw, and saw beyond. They asked questions and often gave the answers to the questions without a word being said. They always welcomed. I never saw them in pique or anger. They pinpointed but enfolded. The hands, too, rarely moved to emphasise, the smile only occasionally developed into laughter out loud. But it convulsed itself by a lowering of the eyelids and a puckering up of every facial muscle. But these were preliminaries, for soon the flood gates of speech would be opened. And what wisdom would then be let loose— a waterfall of English words beautifully spoken.

At first there would be such polite commonplaces as "How nice to see you again," or "Did you have a good journey?", or "I expect you're ready for some tea." He would be reading the latest book of poetry, of travel, of memoirs, of art, for he had wide interests and enormous scholarship. Sooner or later he would take off his spectacles, or look over the top of them, and say, "Have you seen this?" or, "I do think this is good," or, "What a lot about so little." And then, poised over a slice of bread and butter which rarely got eaten, for tea with him was always a kind of masquerade, he would launch straight into what happened to be occupying his mind and interest at the moment. Almost unawares, as if stealing out of the summer dark, would come the inevitable, "I meant to ask you." As he waited for your answer you could almost hear his mind at its questing. Was there ever a more fascinating talker? I have never met one. But he would not allow you to remain silent. The first conversation I ever had with him ended by his stating, with something of a sigh, how disappointed he was that he would never be able to walk along the Great Wall of China. How did he know that I had always wanted to walk along that very wall? Which way would we go? North? South? And what if we met Edmund Blunden half way along? Suppose, suppose. . . . Once he startled me by asking me if I knew the colour of my thoughts. I do not think I gave him a very illuminating answer. Another time he placed his finger on the side of his nose and then, with a mock smile on his face and a deep sepulchral whisper, said, "Behold, I show you a mystery." I waited, half holding my breath. But we never got to what was to be revealed. Instead there began a dissertation on egg cosies which turned itself, in the true de la Mare manner, into an account of his early days with the Anglo-American Oil Company after he had left St. Paul's Cathedral Choir School in 1889. "Where were you then?" he chuckled at me. I wondered if that was the mystery. I remember a talk we had about young children's questions, which soon led on to nursery rhymes and folk songs. Margery Kempe was mentioned, then Traherne, Blake and Edward Thomas; I left him with head whirling.

I have a very special memory of one autumn evening in particular. The Twickenham blinds were drawn and the fire was burning as brightly as it always does in his stories and poems. We sat at heart's ease in the little room which seemed to be his favourite. We had just enjoyed a crumpet tea, or at least I had. There was silence for a while. The fire flickered. The clock ticked. The china cat in the fireplace smiled the same old smile at me and seemed to say, "You'll get nothing and everything out of *him*." He sighed. And then, as if at the first fall of winter snow, Walter de la Mare softly said, "I meant to ask you," and we were away, not too quick and not too slow. We began with some grave comments on the nature of Time, though I did not know that he was working then on his long poem *Wingéd Chariot*. From Time, because of some absurd remark I dropped, we got on to Charles Waterton and his wanderings in South America, and then to John Clare. Something was said about Andrew Young, of whom de la Mare had said, "He watches words like a cat watches a mouse" and then about George Herbert. How did we arrive at nineteenth century aquatints? Why did I find myself displaying ignorance about early English glass? There followed the story of how *Songs of Childhood* was read, and accepted, by Andrew Lang, anecdotes of the visit to America, of his friendships with Thomas Hardy, Katherine Mansfield, Rupert Brooke and Ralph Hodgson, of friends we shared in Gloucestershire and Yorkshire. The fire flickered. The clock ticked. I swear that the cat winked. The last hour of that timeless evening flicked us from Shakespeare to Wilkie Collins, from Rex Whistler to ancient maps, from handwriting to Books of Hours. Before I left he had got back to Time again. And as he said goodbye, with the words, "You'll come again, won't you?" there came the question, "Oh, by the way, do you know why the fire burns?" I began to tell him half-way down the stairs. "But, my dear, you are telling me *how*." And every time I walked away into the dark from that dreaming house, why, why, why, echoed in my ears, with the knowledge that never an unkind thing had been said about anybody, living or dead. Silence, yes, if books and things and people were not appreciated or understood, but never anything unkind. There was always something good to say, even about the smart modern critics of his work, something encouraging, something which summed up the situation generously and compassionately. How he hated the cold spirit and the pomposity of those who always thought they were right. That heart, missed nothing, either. I sometimes wondered if there was ever any end to his learning and remembrance. Over and over I was struck by the fact that he had worked as a writer for sixty years, as hard as any navvy, digging, and breaking down, and building. What hours he had laboured, what inspired beads of sweat had been dropped on how many miles of paper. I believe Walter de la Mare to be a philosopher of the highest order who has had considerable, if unadvertised, influence on the education of young children. One has only to study his great anthology *Early One Morning in the Spring*, to prove this. At eighty-three years of age he was that rare creature, a child of mature years. He knew, with foreknowledge, the inner hearts of children, respecting their innocence but not blinding himself by it. His unity with them was as the touch of dewdrop and rosebud; not for nothing had he had four children and eleven grandchildren. He was, in fact, a practical mystic, who discovered very early on in his life that it was the ugliness of the world which was always threatening to destroy his intimations of immortality.

There is so much more I could write about him, so much more that will come back to me as he gets farther away from me in time. I know how this true and unswerving man accepted life and came to terms with it; I am still amazed by his ranging imagination, his endless questionings and experiments, his letters and kindnesses. If there is any celestial hall for poets, then surely a laurel-crowned easy chair (for how could *he* be comfortable on marble?) is already occupied by him.

He died in June, 1956, and I went to his funeral in St. Paul's where he sang as a boy, and where now my son sings. The poets and writers of England were assembled. His friends were there and his family in undivided force. The Dean welcomed "a child of Paul's" back home. I thought of that other Dean of St. Paul's who wrote:

> For his art did express
> A quintessence even from nothingness.

I came out into the sunlight and thanked the London air for him. But my real goodbyes to him had been said three weeks before he died. "Come again," he said. To that deep, bubbling spring of charmed English water, crystal-pure, I often return.

18 DALES SPRING

SPRING comes slowly to the Yorkshire Dales. Winter seems to last for nearly half the year. The land lies, grey and bare, under sullen skies. It is easy to imagine that a giant is sleeping beneath the folded rock. So it has been since those dim and merciless days when these acres were twisted and pounded into the long valleys and limestone hills, with the water winding its snake-like threads between them.

There are days in this endless winter when the dales are so lonely that even the curlew forsakes them. Valleys and hills are either locked in ice, or blotted out by fog. The valleys seem to be empty of life and sound, and the hills, when they can be seen through the branches of leafless trees, etched out sharply in cold light. Even so, there is a beauty here, classic and austere.

Then there comes a day, quietly and unexpectedly, some-where about the middle of March, when the slumbering giant seems to tire of his prison. He stifles a yawn, stretches him-self and opens his craggy eyes at the first touch of the sun. Then it is that the earth begins to heave and everything puts forth new life. Other days follow, with added signs of returning spring. A dipper gazes at himself in the glassy river, a butterfly tries his unsteady flight across the thistles, a mole mines his nervous way into the pale sun.

There was a day when Spring began to flow in me, when I lived in Leeds. I decided to go walking in Wharfedale. Late in the afternoon I found myself on the road from Burnsall to Bolton Abbey. I rested for a while at the top of a hill which looked out over a wide stretch of open country. Behind me were the dark and menacing trees known as Hagg Wood and, behind the wood, the gently rising slope of Barden Moor. Down the hill to my left was that epitaph of Tudor history known as Burnsall, with its sturdy cottages, graceful bridge, low-browed inn and mullioned Grammar School. To my right, the road continued to wind up the fell through bursting sycamores, greening banks and quickening hedges. And there, straight in front of me, only a mile or so away, the village of Appletree-wick sprawled its stony length across the lower slopes of the hills.

I made a small picture frame of my fingers and looked through it, first into the valley and then at the peaks which surrounded it. Suddenly I realised that my miniature picture frame contained everything that made up Spring in Wharfe-dale. I might have been looking at a Bewick engraving, so accurate, so compressed and so sharply defined was every detail. And the whole had a glow about it which would have excited Turner. Then, for no reason whatever, I found myself repeating the first line of something I had sung so many times in my childhood days. "There is a green hill far away," and there, in Yorkshire, and in reality, was a "green hill", and "far away". And its name was Troller's Gill.

The trees dotted about Troller's Gill and away in the skies on Simon's Seat had so many opening buds on them as to green the air itself. The fields, which quickly dropped from where I was standing, to the river Wharfe beneath, were separated from each other by the craziest patterns of dry walling. Stone-crop was in flower in the little caves in the walls, the ivy-leafed

I

toadflax was shooting out purple tongues, and primroses huddled together, little lemon islands. One or two of the fields, ploughed in winter, showed the first spears of early corn. Another field on the skyline was being harrowed. Plundering gulls streamed behind a man and his toy horses in white, fluttering wake. And other fields which pressed themselves tight up against the old houses and farm buildings of Appletreewick bore on their bare breasts slow moving cloud shadows, pompous rooks and quarrelling crows. Plovers were wheeling out of sun into shade, and a pair of magpies flashed in black and white over the river and back again. At the top of a solitary thorn tree, breaking miraculously into a milk-white cloud, a thrush sang, the dales' loudest trumpeter.

Where the fields seemed to merge themselves with the waters, lambs were crying and dams answering them. These thin cries had not the certainty of the thrush's triumphant song. He welcomed the Spring; the lambs seemed to be shy of it. But they did not cease their crying. Inheritors of the medieval flocks, they gladdened everything that was around them. On his throne, the thrush could see bluebells and anemones drifting their ceaseless tides from Hardington, past Kail Hill and Mill Island, down to the stepping stones at Drebley. And through wondering eyes the lambs watched a hare leap like a thunderbolt from his form in a tuft of grass and race as if he were a wind genie along the curving contours of the hills and then out of sight.

Every sound in that spring-charged air had as background the noise which came from the rushing of the river. It sang joyfully, though not so loudly as the thrush. It danced, pricked out in a dress of waving light, over the shallows and through the rapids, glistening and sparkling, down to the distant sea.

And slung across the slopes to my right were the cottages of Appletreewick, a long string of precious stones let loose on the flowering air. The village lay dreaming that afternoon in its limestone purity. Thin wisps of smoke trailed from a few chimneys and the tired sun was glinting in most of the windows. Somewhere in the distance a hidden waterwheel was drumming away the hours. The village street threaded its uncertain way up to Skyreholme and then lost itself in the wilderness of the moors. I could see one or two children gathering flowers in the meadows. Soon they would return to their homes, bearing in hot hands posies of bluebells, daisies, wilting buttercups and yellow flags in bud, their dark eyes soft and round, chattering their homespun Yorkshire speech like Spring fledglings.

In this land of sheep and stone, of river and hill, ancient man had rubbed his flints together, the Norman had clattered with his armour into its monastic halls, the Dane had pillaged and left his names behind him. For centuries the men who had walked these fields and lived in these cottages had laid up their woollen wealth and then been wrapped in lead and buried six foot deep in Burnsall Church. A Lord Mayor of London first opened his baby eyes on spring fields and crying lambs four hundred years ago. I was seeing the old miracle of Spring rising in Wharfedale as generations before me had seen it stir from solid sleep.

These were some of the things I saw and thought on that April day. As the first stars began to appear over Simon's Seat, a late lark rose into the sky. The thrush had left his tree and flown off farther down the valley. The sheep, with their lambs tagging behind them, were being folded by a boy in clogs and corduroy who, waving stick and arms, drove them, a bleating company, along the river bank. The lark sang on until he became only a song in the evening air. The sun seemed to be drawing the pinkness out of the millstone grit and making the limestone as creamy as the froth upon the river. Camden wrote of the Wharfe, "It runneth with a swift and speedy streame, making a great noise as hee goeth, as if he were froward, stubborne and angry," but on this evening in Spring the river was happy and easy-going.

I climbed higher up the road, remembering how Words-
worth and his sister had trodden it on their way to Bolton
Abbey. Over in Appletreewick, children were being washed
and put to bed in Sandy Gate, Cork Street, and Onion Lane.
The trollers were getting ready to roll down their stones at
midnight and the barghest, that golden dog as big as a bear
and with eyes like saucers, was thinking of leaving his cave
in order to roam the countryside. The stars were shining more
brightly, and the lark had dropped, a silent stone, to the earth.

Spring in Wharfedale is no vulgar fancy. Nature there obeys
the strictest laws of economy. It places most emphasis upon
little points of colour as seen against a rolling expanse of walled
field and wooded hill. It is a Spring compounded of a few singing birds, a parcel of bleating lambs, several handfuls of flowers
and, over all, the great flying clouds. Elsewhere in Yorkshire on
that day looms were working so quickly as to suggest that they
were stealing minutes from time; tall, sooted chimneys casting
broken shadows over dark mills, and light seen only at the
ends of long, straight, cobbled streets. But there in Wharfedale,
a portion of England blessed by Nature and almost unspoiled
by man, the Spring stretched bony fingers from one end of
the valley to the other, lightly warming stone, and stream,
and gently holding in the green palm of its ancient hand,
plaintive lambs and joyful birds.

19 A FIELD IN YORKSHIRE

I SAW the field first when I was walking from Aberford to Tadcaster. That was on a day in early winter when roads and hedges were lightly covered with morning snow. I had been passing and seeing fields all the time. They stretched into the distance on both sides of the road, finally losing themselves on the horizon or disappearing into little valleys and leafless copses. I cannot explain why this particular field caused me to stop and look at it more closely, for it was just an ordinary field. And, even when I looked over the hedge, all I could see was a piece of land that curved over the brow of that hill, a sudden dip down into a gulley, some gulls feeding and, then, a man getting over a gate with a double-barrelled gun under his arm. That, I thought, at the time, was all the impression made on me. And as the weather began to change for the worse and snow started to fall, I left the field behind me, walked down the hill into a village and, eventually, reached Tadcaster.

But I could not get that field out of my mind. I began to see it clearly mirrored in memory's eye. The more I thought about it, the more it began to take possession of me. I knew hundreds of fields and in all parts of the country, but why was *this* field beginning to haunt me? The more I tried to rationalise the situation, the more insistent it became. I found after a few days that I had to stop myself from adding other images to it. Once in a state of trance I placed some Mantegna-like rocks in the middle of the field and a spring of red water gushing up out of the earth and over them. Another time, I imagined that a flock of evil-beaked vultures was squatting round every side of the field like a black imprisoning palisade. There were thousands of them and not one moved. Many times I sketched out the plan of the field on paper, as though the plan itself might explain the feelings I had. I find that when you think about a thing long enough there comes a time when you must act, or end up in a state near demented. I decided to visit the field again, and then, perhaps, to dismiss the whole fancy from my mind.

And so, towards the end of the winter, I began my pilgrimage from Aberford all over again. As I neared the field, which by now I was calling *my* field, I felt an overwhelming desire to sit down on an old mile-stone, and light up a friendly pipe. I began to analyse my feelings. They were a mixture of curiosity, intense depression, and inexplicable fear. I came to the conclusion that I had been overworking. Would it not be better to go back to Leeds and forget all about it? After all, it was just an ordinary field. But other thoughts whispered, "It's no good going home. You will *not* forget it. You cannot forget it." So I braced myself and walked on.

The nearer I got to the field, the more I felt it knew I was coming. It drew me on. It refused to be ignored. It seemed to have chosen *me*, but for what purpose and reason? I could not say. Soon I was looking over the hedge once more. There it lay beneath a grey sky. It had been recently ploughed, and its furrows were full of squabbling rooks. The hedges round its sides were just beginning to bud, the wild arum was sending up its first mysterious sheaths, a chaffinch, suddenly surprised, twittered, and then flashed out of sight. A dog barked on the skyline.

What *was* there about this place which would not let me go? This time I climbed over the hedge, walked down one of the newly-scored furrows, passed through a broken-down gate and came to some twisted thorn trees halfway down a gulley. The farther I got down into the valley, the more depressed I became. A solitary crow eyed me from a flat stone in the middle of an adjacent field and then, leaving what he was tugging at, sailed off clumsily into the wood. Then, suddenly, I came on a tiny beck right at the bottom of the valley, which wound its way along until it vanished from my sight. It made no sound, for all sound seemed to have been choked out of it. New waterweed was beginning to creep out of the banks to make its surface a prisoner and to blot it from the sun. I dipped my fingers into the water. It was deathly cold but, somehow or other, I did not want to take my fingers out. However, after carefully surveying the scene near the beck, I turned my back on it and slowly made my way back to the road. It was quite a steep climb, at an angle I should think of some forty-five degrees. I left a line of bluffs behind me and passed through two cross ridges on either side. The nearer I got to the road the more normal I began to feel, and when I reached the top of the ridge and could see, spreading out before me, the flat plain of York like a great fan, I was convinced that I had allowed myself to fall a victim to hallucinations. Once on the road I gave one last backward glance at the field and then strolled down into the village.

By the time I had reached Tadcaster I remembered the name of the village. It was Towton. I began to wonder where I had heard the name. Hadn't a battle been fought there? I began to think of time theories and of other things. But long before I got to Tadcaster I was convinced that that field *had* been trying to say something to me. Then a most obvious idea struck me.

I looked at an ordnance map, and there it all was. The beck was the little river Cock, the field with the thorn trees the Bloody Meadow, the copse on the brow of the hill Castle Hill Wood. And the map also said that in the field and in neighbouring fields there had been fought on Palm Sunday, 1461, the Battle of Towton.

I now knew that I should have to visit the field for a third time, and on a Palm Sunday. My curiosity had to be satisfied, my daemon to be exorcised for ever.

And so, on the loveliest of Palm Sundays, when every hedge was quick with green budding leaf, when larks were singing over the bright, winter-washed land, and primroses pricking the steep slopes, I looked once more upon the Bloody Meadow and on the lonely valley of the River Cock. For a long time I stood by the gate, just quietly taking in the familiar scene again. Then I began to reconstruct the battle on the spot, for I had been doing some reading about it.

It was certainly the bloodiest battle that Christendom had ever known. On that fatal Sunday the two armies assembled just where I was standing. I had read that on that day the sky was full of snow, with a biting wind blowing from the south. Yorkists and Lancastrians had been getting themselves into position all night, and I thought of them shivering under the stars. The Lancastrians had placed an ambush in Castle Hill Wood; both sides were very confident of victory. Fighting began at 11 o'clock when, poor lost souls, they ought all to have been at church. The snow was still falling, and the wind lashed the blue faces of the Lancastrians. Fauconbridge was the wily leader of the Yorkists, for when the snow started to fall, he ordered his archers to fire a single arrow each, into the enemy's ranks, and then to fall back in good order. The Lancastrians were tricked into firing back, and soon used up all their arrows. Because of the wind and snow, their arrows fell nearly a hundred yards short of their opponents' front line; and all the time the wind was howling, the snow was piling, and over in York Minster they were singing about Him riding on His little donkey, and the people shouting "Hosanna". When the Lancastrians had finished firing, the Yorkist archers quietly stepped forward, picked up the fallen arrows, and put them in their quivers. Which is exactly what the English archers did at Poitiers. But Fauconbridge had told them to leave some arrows where they had fallen, with their cruel shafts sticking into the ground, so that they could be a hindrance to the Lancastrians when they advanced. Both sides had some cannons; the Lancastrians fired off theirs early in the proceedings. But the Yorkist artillery, under the command of the Earl of Norfolk, had not yet appeared on the scene. Their cannons were still being dragged across the river Aire at Ferrybridge.

Just after mid-day the Lancastrians started to advance. They charged down the hill at which I was looking, with all their billmen and spearmen. Many got impaled on the arrows. They all found the snow a hindrance, for it drove straight into their faces. The Yorkists met this charge by firing Lancastrian arrows at them first of all, and then let loose their own. The advancing army suffered terrible losses, but as fast as one man fell, another took his place. They found it very difficult to stand in that rain of snow, but slowly they pressed on, a great seething, solid wedge of men. At this point Fauconbridge ordered the Yorkist bowmen to retire to the rear, for they were tired out and had used up all their arrows. Then hand-to-hand fighting began. I thought I could hear it again echoing down the centuries. Axe upon axe, spear upon spear, blood spouting out on to the trampled snow. I pictured a wall of bleeding bodies, a wall which got gradually higher and higher. This was a Palm Sunday air, full of snow and murder. And I could hear those faraway dying men screaming for God's mercy.

They fought like this for the best part of two hours; it looked as if the Lancastrians were going to win. But in the middle of the afternoon the snow ceased, and Norfolk's men began to appear on the Yorkist's right flank. They had come just in time, but they had to wade through fallen snow and through all the little rivulets of blood which, fanwise, trickled like a thousand outstretched hands, down the valley into the river.

Fighting went on until sunset, with no quarter given on either side. But just when the light began to fail, Norfolk's reinforcements began to turn the tide of battle in favour of the Yorkists. As the sun began to set, its dying rays picked out Norfolk sitting bolt upright on his gaily-caparisoned dapple grey and the figure of Fauconbridge who, bare-headed, watched the Lancastrians in retreat. They ran in terror away from The Bloody Meadow and made for Tadcaster, but they did not retreat to safety. When they got to the river Cock they were trapped. The snow had made the water there nearly six feet deep, and the river was running very swiftly. The Yorkists started to chase them like so many hounds at bay, and killed many at the ford. Once again the Lancastrian dead made a toppling wall of corpses. The river was spanned by a score of bridges, and every bridge was made of dead men. When night at last fell, and Palm Sunday was over, the fields where I was now standing were strewn with thirty thousand dead bodies, blood was seeping into the earth, mangled horses and men stared up at unfriendly stars. So ended the battle of Towton Moor.

I knew now why the field had haunted me. I knew what it had to say to me. I had been sitting in The Bloody Meadow itself, where the greatest slaughter had taken place. I had been surrounded by the dying, who could not remain quiet. I slowly rose to my feet again, got to the main road and, shaken to my depths, walked back to Aberford. The sun dropped down behind the Palm Sunday hills. A blackbird whistled over the peaceful land. History and death had spoken to me from the earth itself.

20 THE FRENCH SOLDIER

I WORKED in Plymouth during the last war. But what I have to tell of those grim years is not of the destruction of the city, when bombs fell out of the Devon sky like thunderbolts, or of children being evacuated, or of battered warships limping home across the Sound. It is the story of a very strange meeting, of a friendship made on impulse, of two people whose lives crossed and recrossed. When I think of it now it is as if it had never been, as if I had dreamt it all.

On a bright and calm morning in June 1940, after a blazing night of terror, I found myself on Plymouth Hoe. France had fallen a few days before. It seemed as if the air itself had been bludgeoned into silence. Down on the various quays soldiers were being landed from overcrowded troopships. I watched them making their weary way up the grassy slopes of the Hoe to be re-formed into their various units before marching off to the rest camps. It was as if I was present at some kind of strange play. I remember how moved I was at the sight of those straggling files, how very frightened, too. It is nearly a quarter of a century ago but I can still picture the scene—the knapsacks the men carried, the unshaven, strained faces, the crumpled uniforms, the dream-like silence.

Although ignorant of military matters I soon knew that the soldiers being landed that morning were French. Some inner urge prompted me to walk down to one of the quays to be an even closer spectator of what was now happening. I stood quietly on one side as soldier after soldier passed me by. I lit a cigarette, as diverse thoughts crowded into my head. So the French, in retreat, had invaded England after all. Hardy would have liked that one. Was this the end of the war then? Should I next see Germans landing in triumph on the Plymouth quays? But my reflections were suddenly halted.

One of the Frenchmen stepped out of the file, came over to me, and asked me if I could give him a cigarette. I understood the request and gave him one. He smiled and thanked me when I handed him my own cigarette so that he could light his. He puffed away with obvious relief.

The more I think about the incident now the odder I think it is. Out of all those Frenchmen why should that one approach me on foreign soil and beg a cigarette? Why pick on me?

I walked by the soldier's side to the top of the Hoe. We chatted together, he in broken English and I in bad French, until his company was ready to move off. I now had time to study him more closely. He was younger and taller than I, in his twenties, I should think. The unshaven face was long and sallow with high cheekbones and deepset, incredibly-dark eyes. There was a crescent-shaped scar over the left eye. The thin moustache which hid a sensitive upper lip was clearly a permanent feature. The strong, tapering fingers were badly tobacco-stained. The only other thing I learned about him was that he was a medical student. With only a year to go at the medical school at Bordeaux he had been called to the colours. We did not even exchange names and addresses. After we had shaken hands and made a few more pleasant exchanges, the unit, a company of Engineers, I gathered, was brought to attention, and then quick-marched away.

I made my way back to the centre of the town by a side

street, unbelievably moved by the experience. Suddenly I felt very close to the war. I thought a great deal about the French soldier for many weeks after. I didn't think I should ever see him again. But time was going to prove me wrong.

I left Plymouth just before the war ended. And in the early 1950's I paid a visit to Sark to fall under the spell of that enchanted channel island. I decided to write a book about it which, eventually, I did. I called it *Sark Discovered*; it found a publisher and was well received. Now when I was writing it I had to read a great deal about the long and involved history of the island and this entailed a brief visit to France. I stayed in the village of Canisy about halfway between Coutances and St. Lô, learning what I could about the de Carterets who had been the first Seigneurs of Sark. I put up at the local guest house, kept by one Madame Flamand, visited the manor where the de Carterets had once lived, the churchyard where they were buried, and consulted a number of old documents.

I woke up on the morning of my last day at Canisy feeling far from well. Had I drunk too much of the vin du pays? Was it that Calvados the curé had given me at Coutances? Or had there been something in Madame's soup to upset me? I certainly did not fancy the coffee and croissants that morning. Instead, I made my uncertain way to the doctor's, a certain Martin Ombré, I was told, who had not been in the district very long. He lived in Canisy but held surgeries in three other neighbouring villages.

I sat in Dr. Ombré's surgery with half a dozen other patients, all clearly known to each other, but all sitting dour and silent. They eyed me suspiciously. I was nearly overcome by the smell of their garlic-laden breaths. But at last it was my turn to go in.

I recognised him at once. It was my Frenchman. I should have known him even if I had not spotted the scar over his left eye. He had filled out somewhat and looked very smart in a pin-striped lounge suit. But he did not recognise *me* until, having listened to my tale of woe and diagnosed that I had picked up the current germ that was ravaging the countryside, he looked at me intently and said, "Monsieur, I seem to know your face. Have we not met before?" I laughed and at once enlightened him. He put his hands on my shoulders and said, "Sit down, sit down, mon ami. Have a cigarette." And he pushed a box of Caporals under my nose.

He then gave me a draught of some medicine which he said would soon clear up my trouble and, there and then, insisted that I should go back home with him and stay quietly there until he had finished his rounds. Then he would join me for lunch. I told him I did not want any lunch but that I would go with him.

Martin Ombré had not long been married. While he was away I lay on a chaise longue in their best sitting-room, chatting with his young wife, a charming, ebullient creature, not beautiful, but very striking-looking, and full of good French common sense. Yes, she told me, Martin had come safely through the war, had been allowed to leave the army to complete his medical training in 1943, had qualified a year later, they had met at a friend's house, had married in 1945 and now had a young son who was also called Martin. He was spending the day with his grandmother at St. Lô. Martin had been an assistant to an old doctor in Coutances until 1949; they had been in Canisy for three years.

The story was straightforward and commonplace enough but all the same I wondered by what trick of fate Martin Ombré and I had been thrown together again. And if there was a purpose behind it all.

I spent the rest of the day with the Ombrés and was certainly feeling much better by the evening when I took, on doctor's orders, a little thin soup and a glass of Epernay. Martin and I talked of everything under the English and French suns until it was time for me to walk back with him to Madame Flamand's. I left Canisy the next morning.

Martin and I kept in touch with each other for a couple of

years and then the letters between us got fewer and fewer.
After all said and done, we had few common interests and
knew little of each other at first hand. I was always promising
myself that I would go back to see him at Canisy. But I never
did. I do remember though that I sent him a copy of my book
about Sark.

Then, a few years ago, I had occasion to visit my own doctor.
By now I was living in London. I didn't go to see him because
I was ill; I wanted to discuss another matter with him. I waited
in his surgery glancing casually at the magazines littered
about the room. I had worked my way down one pile and was
about to begin on another when my eye fell on a French newspaper. What is more it was a local newspaper, published from
Coutances. I wondered what a provincial French newspaper
was doing in my doctor's surgery until I recalled that he had
recently enjoyed a motoring holiday in Europe. Then I realised
that the paper might carry some news of Canisy. Indeed it did.
For I read with horror at the bottom of one of the columns the
following caption; *Sudden Death of Local Doctor*. I read on.
Martin Ombré had been drowned while on holiday on the
coast of Brittany. There were the usual details of his career and
of his funeral. I was deeply affected by it all and could not
explain why once again I felt myself suddenly very close to a
war that had been dead for so long.

I did not tell my own doctor any of this. I had my interview
with him and then, subdued and deeply disturbed, went back
home. But as I left his surgery he looked up at me and said,
"By the way, don't you think you are smoking too much?"
And this simple statement completely shattered me. I thought
of that morning on Plymouth Hoe, of Martin asking me for a
cigarette, of Martin giving me a cigarette in Canisy, of Martin,
safely landed from the sea in 1940, drowned in it fifteen years
later. Surely this should have been the end of the French
soldier for me. Not so.

I was recently invited to a gathering of young French

students doing various courses in this country. It was a large and gay party. I found myself next to a tall, dark-haired, solemn youth, about seventeen or eighteen, I should say, who was hoping to become a teacher. He had only just left the university. He was anxious to know from what part of England I came because my accent intrigued him. When I told him, he said he was from the country, too. "A villager, like you," he said. "And the name of your village?" I asked. "O, you will have never heard of it," the boy said. "It is a tiny place between Coutances and St. Lô. It is called Canisy." "And your name?" I replied, as he offered me a cigarette. I was not surprised when he said, "Martin Ombré." But I doubt if he understood why there were tears in my eyes when he leaned across and lit the cigarette for me, and why my hands were trembling.

I suppose I ought to have told the boy the whole story. But I did not. And I do not think I shall ever see him again.

21 A GLOUCESTERSHIRE TRAGEDY

I ONCE had a friend who was Head Mistress of a village school in north Gloucestershire. Shortly before she retired I went to see her. I wanted to congratulate her on having worked so patiently and so successfully in that remote school for nearly forty years.

When I arrived, the children had already gone home. The long schoolroom with its high, ecclesiastical windows, in which the older children were taught, was empty but for the care-taker's wife who was silently sweeping the floor. A clock, with white and vacant face, ticked solemnly away on the pink-distempered wall. A highly-coloured and dramatic picture of the landing of the Romans in Britain looked down on us and seemed to mock the stillness of the room. There was the smell of chalk in the air.

My friend was in the schoolhouse next door busily getting

K   143

the tea. We greeted each other boisterously as we had done for thirty years. Then I helped her carry the tea things out on to the small lawn at the back of the house. There we sat and talked, and sipped our tea, in the glow of the late September sun, until falling dew and fading light drove us indoors. First leaves were already floating slowly down, one by one, on to the cold, flat gravestones in the churchyard beyond the school wall.

My friend knew of my great interest in old school log books and of my fascination for everything Victorian. So that night, as I lolled at my ease before the first fire of the season, a glass of home-made dandelion wine at my elbow, she produced one of the school's log books I had never seen before. It covered the years 1889-1895. The fat, leather-covered, slightly-mildewed book lay in my warm lap. I opened it and began to turn its thick pages, bringing the oil lamp a little nearer to do so. I soon discovered that a Miss Mary Amelia Black had been Head Mistress of the school for the whole period covered by the book. I had a picture of her, stiff and starched, with long skirt, and hair packed at the back of her head in a tight bun. In imagination, I heard her calling the register and marshalling the children as they clattered into school from the rough playground.

At first there did not seem to be anything very unusual about any of the entries. I had read them a hundred times before in many such log books. There were the usual references to the annual visit of H.M.I., the weekly visits of the squire's wife, and the almost daily appearance of the parson. There were, I learned, fairly constant changes in the babies' room; the reading books had arrived a whole month late in the autumn of 1891; the children had been entertained by the squire in his park on the occasion of a royal marriage; the winter of 1893 was exceptionally hard and the attendance exceptionally low. I was fascinated by some of the names of the children and wondered what had happened to them. Was

Nehemiah Huggins still living? Had Hagar Perkins got married? Did William Nutgrove ever learn to read?

But my pulses began to quicken when I got to the year 1894. There was an entry for the 4th September of that year, written, as usual, in Miss Black's impeccable copperplate hand. It read quite simply, "Emma Green began as a pupil teacher today."

A few pages farther on I came across this, "Emma Green was late today. Had to speak to her sharply." And for the next few months there were regular references to the behaviour of Emma Green. She was obviously something of a problem. But I was conjuring up a picture of her. She became for me, even at that stage, the counterpart of a character in a Hardy novel. I was sure that she was short, neatly-made, passionate, and hot-tempered. It was very clear that she had fallen foul of Miss Black, for there followed a succession of critical entries about her. "Emma Green absent from school today"; "Emma Green did not know the lines from *Paradise Lost* for the Inspector"; "Emma Green very sulky all the afternoon"; "Must speak to Emma Green's mother about her"; "Spoke to the Vicar this morning about Emma Green." Emma had become an obsession with Miss Black. There was bad feeling between them. As I sat there with my friend I could almost hear the harsh words stabbing the quiet air in the schoolroom next door. Yet I could not understand why I was getting so worked up about it all. I reminded myself that I had never known these two people. And their squabbles must have been so trivial.

There was a final reference to Emma Green on the 7th July, 1894. To my surprise, and amusement, it was written in red ink. And these were the words I read, "Had to send for the Rev. Fortescue this afternoon. When he came I had to tell him that Emma Green had insulted me in front of the children and that either she or I would have to leave. I cannot write down here what she called me. I have written the words on a separate piece of paper. I have placed it in an envelope at the back of this book. Rev. Fortescue was very angry with Emma Green and told her to go home and never come back to school again."

My friend gave me another glass of wine. But I had almost forgotten time and place as, with trembling fingers, I turned to the back of the log book. Yes, there was the envelope. But it had been opened. Other eyes had read the words before me. Fortunately, though, the piece of folded paper was still inside. I took it out, unfolded it, and read the fatal words, "Emma Green said, 'You are a silly bitch.'" My first reaction was to burst out laughing. I bet, I thought to myself, that old harridan of a schoolmistress had deserved it. I was certain that she had led that poor young girl a dance. But for what quite illogical and inexplicable reasons did I range myself on Emma Green's side? I did not once ever think that Miss Black's patience must have been sorely tried, that in Emma Green she had caught a little tartar.

I closed the book and said goodbye to my friend. I stepped out into the dark, holding a bunch of late roses which she had given me to take home to my wife. She had offered to lend me the old log book. But I had read all I wanted to.

But I could not get Emma Green out of my head. Somehow or other I just could not leave her all by herself, walking sadly back to her father's cottage on that far away July afternoon. She had been dismissed from her post. She would never become a teacher. I knew that I should have to find out more about her.

The following year I wrote to my friend again. She had now left the school for good and was living in her own cottage on the outskirts of the village. I asked her if I could come and see her. She wrote back at once, "I know why you want to come. I have some information for you here."

A week or so later I stood in my friend's kitchen and watched her getting the tea. We greeted each other more soberly on this occasion. "I know why you are here," she said. "I haven't known you all these years for nothing. After tea you had better go along and have a word with old Rupert Nash, the landlord of *The Greyhound*. He will tell you a lot about Emma

Green. He knew her. And you had better stay the night here."

It was rather a sombre tea time. My friend knew that I was itching to be off. She came to the gate and showed me the chimneys of *The Greyhound* through the trees a few fields away. They were cutting the hay as I walked through the meadows, the pitchers silhouetted against the evening sky. And the words of the old song came into my mind,

> O the green grass is cut,
> The long days are over,
> My lover has gone.
> I am fading away
> Where the meadows once shone
> With the grass and the clover.

Rupert Nash was drinking a pint of his own cider when I stepped into the bar parlour of his public house. He was a well-preserved, hearty-looking man, with a fine, white beard. I put him down as being about sixty-five or so. It turned out that he was in his seventy-eighth year. I soon got into conversation with him for he had been expecting me. There was no one else in the parlour at the time for the night was young.

"So you knew Emma Green," I ventured. He did not answer immediately. Then he took another swig of his cider, sighed, and said, "Poor Emma. I was in love with her, you know. But she would have none of me. She was a bit of a handful, I can tell you. Her father and mother were most respectable people. He was the Vicar's gardener. She was a beauty, too. Short, with dark, darting eyes. Had a frightful temper, though. Was always wandering off by herself. They tried to make a teacher of her. But she would have none of that. She got on the wrong side of Miss Black who was the schoolmistress then. Hard old thing *she* was. But come down with me to the acre tomorrow. I am going to start on the scything." I could get nothing more out of him. And, in any case, the place began to fill up.

Rupert called for me the next morning. The sun was already high in the heavens. The hay-makers were still at it. When we got to the churchyard the dew was off the grasses, peacock butterflies were fluttering round the buddleias, dusty bees were hard at work in the moss roses. Rupert first took his long-handled scythe from where it was fastened to the wall in the belfry tower. Then I followed him to the far side of the church-yard. When he stopped he solemnly took off his wide-brimmed straw hat and pointed to a grave only a few feet away from an Irish yew. He began to read the words on the headstone out loud.

Emma Green aged 17 years
Youngest daughter of James and Mercy Green
of this parish
Born 16 September 1879
Found drowned in Church Brook 7 July 1896

That was all. I felt the blood drain from my face. Found drowned. Then my heart began to beat wildly as I suddenly realised that I was standing by Emma Green's grave with Rupert Nash who had actually known her and that the date was the 7th July, though sixty years later.

Rupert leaned upon his scythe, looking as if he were a cari-cature of Father Time, and went on with the details of the tragic story. "When the school got rid of her," he said, "she stayed at home for a time helping her mother. She would have nothing to do with any of us in the village. She was never seen inside the church again. I *did* ask her one day to come with me to Barton Fair at Gloucester but she tossed her head and said, 'What, with *you*?' Sometimes I used to meet her walking in the fields or wandering by Church Brook. Then she disappeared altogether. No one knew what had happened to her. But it soon came out that she had run away from home and was living up in London."

The old man stopped at this point and viciously lopped off

the heads of some of the tallest grasses. Then he began scything the rest, with sure and steady motion. But I knew there was more to come. He was taking his time. After a while Rupert propped his scythe against the gnarled trunk of the yew and led me by the hand to the small wooden wicket gate in the long, grey church wall. At the bottom of the slope, hidden by over-hanging trees, I could hear Church Brook gurgling along its flashing pebbles.

We leant on the wall, both of us clutching our hats. Rupert began again. "Yes, she walked to Tewkesbury and got the train to London. I missed her terribly. It was as if she had gone to China. I didn't think I'd ever see Emma again. I did, though. She stayed in London for about a year and then she came back home as suddenly as she had gone. Nobody saw much of her. Then it leaked out that she was going to have a baby. She wouldn't say who the father was. Old Fortescue couldn't get anything out of her. And Miss Black was reported as saying, 'I am not at *all* surprised.' Well, it was true enough. Emma had her baby. It was a boy. She called him Job. But she never had him christened."

Rupert put his hands over his eyes. His voice, by now, had dropped to a whisper. A coldish breeze shook all the leaves in the trees. I looked up and saw a heron flying over the church tower. Then Rupert spoke again. "Emma got a job on one of the farms. But soon after she disappeared again leaving the baby with her father and mother. They were at their wits' end, I can tell you. Everybody said she'd cleared off to London again. 'To walk the streets, no doubt,' said Miss Black. But we were all wrong. My father had *The Greyhound* then, sir. One evening when the bar was full and the cider was flowing I was helping father in the taproom. Tim Cotter from the forge suddenly rushed in with the news that Emma Green had been found drowned in Church Brook. They had just fished her out. Some children, who had been playing there had seen her floating down the stream with her black hair stretched out behind

her. Several of us dashed out and made our way across the
fields to the Brook. I was the first to get there. And I helped
to carry her through this gate. And we trundled her back
home on the bier."

By now the old man was in tears. They were floating down
his white beard. I was not far from tears, either. I left him to
his memories and scything and made my way back, shaken to
the heart, to my friend's house. She had known the whole
story but wanted me to hear it from Rupert's lips.

And there the incident would have ended for me though I
sometimes wondered what had happened to little Job. I did not
ever go back to the north Gloucestershire village again for my
friend moved away from it soon afterwards. Then she wrote
to tell me that Rupert Nash had died and that strangers had
taken over *The Greyhound*. There was a new Head Mistress
at the school too who was a charmer. The children were devoted to her.

But the story has a strange sequel which makes me wonder
if we ever really know anything at all about life and its laby-
rinthine ways.

Not long ago I was speaking to a gathering of teachers. At
lunch I found myself sitting next to a merry, short, dark-haired,
black-eyed little beauty. Her accent betrayed that she was from
my county of Gloucestershire. "Where are you from?" I asked
her. "From near Tewkesbury," she smiled. "Have *you* ever
been there?" "Many times," I said. "Well," she went on, "my
father is a nurseryman there. You may have heard of him. Job
Green. I'm his only daughter." "And your name?" I said. I
knew what her answer would be. But I did not move a muscle
when she nodded her head and said, "Emma Green, sir."

22 A FOOL IN THE FOREST

AND now I stand on the hill of Highgate as once I stood on my childhood hills in Gloucestershire. But it is not the distant Severn I see curling through the gleaming meadows of summer, nor the white cathedral tower of Gloucester standing out plain and sharp against the ragged background of the Cotswolds, but the whole wide expanse of London, another river, no meadows, but many towers.

But I am near enough to trees and woodlands to feel no acute sense of deprivation. There are, to begin with, four trees in my own small garden, budding to plan, at the appropriate season of the year. These trees are no more than two aged ornamental planes and two rather dull prunuses. But they are trees. When these do not satisfy, there are the Highgate Woods and Kenwood within walking distance, the last surviving witnesses of the ancient and ruined forest of Middlesex.

It is not so long since, either, that I went to see a flock of sheep running free on Parliament Hill Fields, and spoke to their cockney shepherd; a morning or so later, I saw a fox slink away, as bold as red brass, from where he had been sipping the cold water of the White Stone Pond on Hampstead Heath. I knew that he had his den in one of the decayed Victorian vaults in Highgate Cemetery. Until recently, there was one pair of badgers, at least, still undisturbed in their holt among the trees at Kenwood, buttercups, too, on the Heath, and a hidden stream where my children and I could gather handfuls of tea-time watercress every June. Acorns fall each October in Highgate Woods, as they fell every autumn for me in the Forest of Dean, and where they will fall again, this year, and next in the long glades at Speech House. Acorns are symbols, not of nostalgia, but of continuance; they look forwards, not backwards, so that my children now inherit the woods of my childhood by enjoying their own London woods with me.

I have lately been back to the Forest of Dean after a gap of years. It is generally supposed that it is unwise, if one is to avoid disappointment, to return to the place of one's infancy once it has been left for good. Everything, say those who have tried it, will be different. Everything will be smaller and insignificant, familiar landmarks will have gone, friends and acquaintances dead or scattered, or, if still living on where they have always been, so changed as to be almost a new race of people.

But I was not disappointed. I found that some of the copses and rides of the Forest were indeed gone, that there were shorn wastelands where once had been singing avenues of trees. But in other places, where there had been baby plantations when I was a boy, the trees have become giants and were as lovely as growing trees can be. Too many conifers, perhaps, and fewer birds, but still glorious lines of beeches and oak trees, outfacing Time. And everywhere holly bushes, as if it were always Christmas in the Forest of Dean.

The Severn, too, continues to flow serenely out to sea. There is no longer a ferry at Newnham, but there are still elvers in season, the Bore as high a wall of terrifying water as ever, the evening sun, blood-red on the stream at Broad Oak, and children dabbling. I chatted with a gipsy-like girl who was playing on the banks with her younger brother. "We bin told not to go in the water," she offered, "it be dangerous." I thought immediately of that other slim, dark-eyed creature I had watched being lifted, limp and bloodless, out of Severn all those years ago, her hair a dripping mat of weed and foam, the life bubbling out of her. My gipsy child went on, the ripe Forest of Dean speech warm on her prattling tongue, "A boat smashed up the Severn Bridge. But they be going to build another." So it was going to be all right, then.

I waved her goodbye when I began to make my slow way up the long dragging hill from Newnham to Cinderford. How often had I made that same four-and-a-half-mile journey with my mother on our picnicking way to Severn, or back home with baskets of gold-flecked September plums. How often had I stepped it out with Will Harvey, poetry and Gloucestershire marrying in the cloudless air, hedges quick with springtime or thick and flowery with the dower of summer. And I chuckled to myself as I remembered that glowing day when I had scuttled up this same winding hill with a French general's pound note in my Red Cross tin.

And so I came back to the cottage where I had been brought up. It had not greatly changed and it still felt like home. Later, I walked down the road where I had spent so many innocent Saturday nights with my friends, past the church where my family had worshipped for years and where I had been a chorister, and so to the Market Place. Here the fairs and the travelling theatre had stood but now that enraptured plot of land had been built on, and its past barely remembered. But the little town of Cinderford was much the same as I had experienced it in my childhood, though cleaner and more prosperous. Some of the names over the shops were unchanged. I met a few old and welcoming friends but most of the faces in the streets only reminded me of their ancestors. There were ghosts at every corner. Yet, oddly enough, I felt no great emotion about it all. Cinderford had never been a beautiful place. It had been carved out of the woodland less than 150 years ago and had all the grimness of a Victorian creation. But I had lived in this place for over a third of my life, I had had a breathing space there, before I moved away. I think now that I must always have been a looker-on at its life rather than an active participator in it. I felt no inner compulsion to go back and live there again, to rediscover original springs, in the hope of finding some newly-born spiritual satisfaction. Not that I felt ungrateful or critical or blasé. I was neither depressed nor elated. In fact, I realised, as I strolled about the narrow streets, that for years I had carried my own security with me. I had no need to search for it in Cinderford, or anywhere else.

I walked over land that had once carried green woodland on its back, on whose root-bound paths I had so many times trudged to the little squat church at the end of it which we had always called the Forest Church. I missed the trees acutely. I felt naked, with all my feelings exposed, as it were, to alien air. Uneasily and unhappily, I came to the graveyard where my mother had lain buried for a quarter of a century. I had often come to that grassy tomb in the past with, and without, her, with, because her husband was buried there, and my foster brother who had died in a military hospital in the Great War. She and I used to bring flowers to this tomb every Palm Sunday. Then it was that we looked at all the other graves while she told me secret and private things about some of those who lay mouldering in the Forest clay. We were paying our respects to the dead. We commented on how tidy this grave was, how neglected that, what had happened to this trades-man, what kind of a woman this long-liver had been, how this child had never spoken a word but had suddenly died in its cot. We brought the dead to life on Palm Sunday afternoons, not morbidly, but as if, once again, they were walking the world with us. The white flowers in our hands were votive offerings. We were experiencing both the Resurrection and the Life.

So here I was again in the Forest churchyard but in what a wilderness of lank grasses; the rain-washed marble crosses and cracked headstones raised their neglected words of love and hope to Heaven. I trampled through wet tangles looking for mother's grave. At last, I found it, with a deep sense of guilt that I had not visited it more often. I read the words on the surrounding stone, her name, by the side of her husband's and son's, the years of their births and deaths, all withering away into corruption. I knelt there alone on a bleak hillside, overcome with thankfulness and memory, love and hope flowing between us, fire and water, nothing divided. I was oblivious to the wilderness of grass and the neglect of stone. I was at peace with the names written there, with the overgrown tombs. I was part of a unity for which I could find no explanation. Beyond the crumbling walls of the graveyard the ruddled sheep were running wild. The red bus to Gloucester snorted up the hill. I caught a glimpse of the grey-haired driver. I had taught him in school forty years ago.

I also went to see a friend I had not seen for many years. We had been at school together at Monmouth, William Jones's scholars, poor boys educated by the Worshipful Company of the Haberdashers. He offered to take me in his battered car into the depths of the Forest so that I could stand again on the Roman road at Blackpool Bridge, that charmed bit of it, still left uncovered, of the thin diameter which ran right across the Forest to the important iron settlement at Ariconium. On our way we stopped for a drink at the pub where "our Glad" and "Perce" had once worked. I smiled at the remembrance of their outlandish wedding. But Gladys and her father had been dead for a dozen years, and Percy had moved out, with his sorrow, back to his native Wales. I wondered what he looked like now, if he ever gave a passing thought to the capers they had all cut on that fantastic day. Now we were served by strangers from Yorkshire. They came from the Dales and were itching to get back to them.

When, at last, we got to the Roman road, we stared at it in sober silence. What, then, was so moving about it? Why did this particular piece of landscape draw us together and back over the years? The Roman road. What had this to do with the Latin we had learned at Monmouth School? And all those translations from Ovid and Caesar? And Sammy Littlewood trying to drive North and Hillard into our thick Forest skulls? "What a fool you are," he had said. Yes, I thought now, a fool from the Forest. The Roman coins found not far from the road seemed to bring us much nearer to the living Roman, the marching legions, especially that lovely gold coin of Vespasian which the plough had turned up at St. Briavels.

I looked at my friend. There he was, a man in his late fifties, rotund, square-shouldered, solid on his big feet, slow moving as he had always been, but eye undulled and mind as questing as ever.

We walked for an hour among the trees near the road. I looked at them with my fifty-year-old face but it was my seventeen-year-old face which smiled back at me. I mused for a while. When I was seventeen there was no bomb to scare us. That was still to come. We did not know much about the social problems of our day. Perhaps we were social problems and did not know it. We were too ignorant of the misery and hunger in the world. Certainly we were not miserable and there was always something to eat, however meagre. Perhaps we relied too much on our sense of wonder, our belief in happy and enduring things, smug, no doubt, but innocent. As a matter of fact, we all believed we should live out our days in the Forest of Dean. So we took life as it came, giving little thought for the morrow. Not that my particular world was at all cosy or

romantic. I had no rich friends or relations; there were no
state grants towards my further education. Of course, I was
well aware of the bad housing conditions in the Forest, the
rotten, water-infested pits, the lack of opportunity for many
who would have benefited, and of gasping miners fighting for
breath enough to keep them going, and of families far worse
off than ours. I hated these things. They were at hand and we
couldn't escape them. I despised those who had been responsible for them but I had little love for the slick, power-seeking
local politicians. All the same, I did not want to tread anyone
down so that I might get to the top, or behave as if I owned my
neighbour, or think that I had got all the answers off pat. At
seventeen I just wanted to enjoy what was to be enjoyed—the
Forest itself, my friends, poetry, music, books, flowers. I suppose I must have been a simple-minded creature with a lot of
obsolete values.

I am still that seventeen-year-old boy at heart. I carry around
with me such memories as the sunlight on Severn, I can hear
the trees talking in Abbotswood, I plough my way, in imagination, through the young snow that, once a year, used to block
all the roads from Cinderford to Gloucester. I feel far from
smug. I am grateful. And I am blessed. I do not spurn the
bounty which life has given me in such full measure. If I had
a drum I would beat it to show how fortunate I am.

Last summer, my wife and I, with our children, were sitting
on the lawn of our Highgate house. My son and I were reading
in the shade of the trees; my daughter was sun-worshipping
with her mother. The borders were loud with dusty bees
plundering the heavy foxgloves growing among the cool ferns
on the rockery, descendants of those which had been sent to
us from the Forest and from Wharfedale. The tiny apron of a
lawn looked green and very pleasant for I had cut and watered
it the night before. Occasionally a drowsy bird twittered and
a cabbage white butterfly floated over one garden fence, and
then over another. It was a commonplace domestic scene. We

might have been marooned on a green island in the country-side of Nowhere.

But it was then that I realised how life comes to its full circle and what a strange journey it had been from all the trees in the Forest of Dean to the four in my town garden.

And what am I as the result of it all? Lunatic, lover, or poet? All three, perhaps, because I am of imagination all compact. I have certainly seen a few of the earth's devils, admired Helen's beauty on many a brow, and on one in particular, and never found it very difficult to suppose that a bush was a briar. The glory, for all that some of its bloom has been rubbed off, has remained. So that, when, at lights out I find, another forest to explore, that

> unfathomable deep
> Forest where all must lose
> Their way,

I may well discover, as Edward Thomas did, that only in *its* shades

> love ends—
> Despair, ambition ends.
> All pleasure and all trouble.